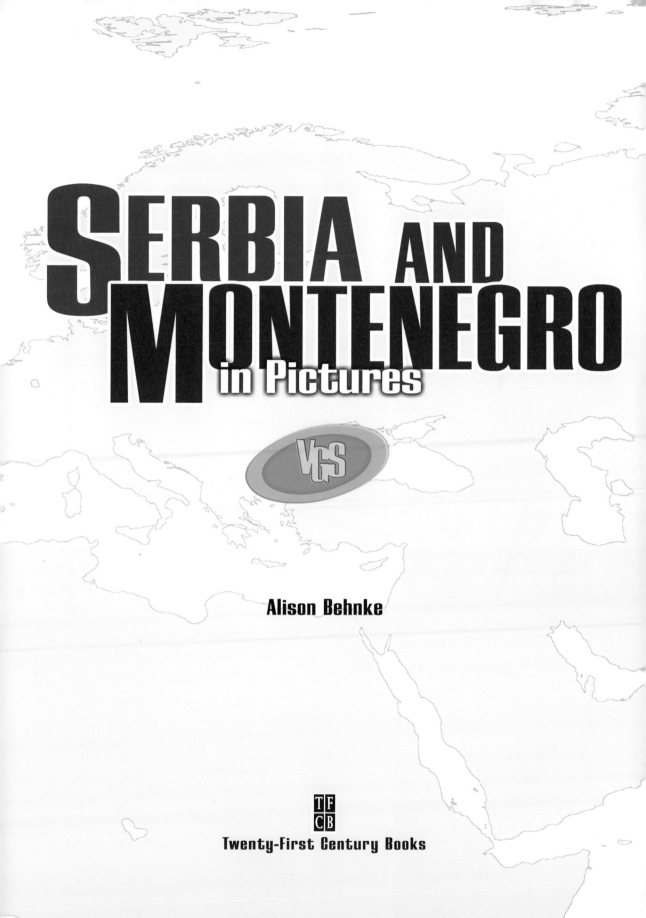

SERBIA AND MONTENEGRO
in Pictures

Alison Behnke

TF
CB
Twenty-First Century Books

Contents

Website address: www.lernerbooks.com

Twenty-First Century Books
A division of Lerner Publishing Group
241 First Avenue North
Minneapolis, MN 55401 U.S.A.

Library of Congress Cataloging-in-Publication Data

Behnke, Alison.
    Serbia and Montenegro in pictures / by Alison Behnke.
        p. cm. — (Visual geography series)
    Includes bibliographical references and index.
    ISBN-13: 978-0-8225-2679-7 (lib. bdg. : alk. paper)
    ISBN-10: 0-8225-2679-4 (lib. bdg. : alk. paper)
    1. Serbia and Montenegro—Pictorial works—Juvenile literature. I. Title. II. Visual geography series
DR1942.B44 2007
    949.710022'2—dc22
                                                                        2005035155

Manufactured in the United States of America
1 2 3 4 5 6 – BP – 12 11 10 09 08 07

INTRODUCTION

Serbia and Montenegro is an Eastern European federation made up of two former Yugoslav republics. Home to more than 10 million people, it was formed in the wake of a long and brutal conflict that tore Yugoslavia apart in the 1990s and early 2000s. The war and the vicious ethnic and religious violence that accompanied it inflicted deep scars on the land and its people, leaving thousands dead, wounded, and homeless. Because of this recent history, many modern observers think of the country as a place of violence, hatred, and suffering. The southern region of Kosovo—where some of the war's worst atrocities took place—has become an especially well-known symbol of the young federation's struggles.

However, the land that makes up modern Serbia and Montenegro has a long history, stretching back thousands of years before the recent wars that brought it such unhappy fame. That history was not always peaceful, either. It was marked by frequent invasions and conquests by outsiders. The invaders included the armies of the ancient Roman

Empire, the Byzantine Empire, and the Ottoman (Turkish) Empire. A series of conflicts known as the Balkan Wars began in the early 1900s. World War I (1914–1918)—a great conflict that shattered the region—quickly followed.

World War II (1939–1945) was equally devastating. It took the lives of thousands and left the homes, farms, and factories of what was then Yugoslavia in ruins. From World War II's destruction rose the powerful new leader Josip Broz, known as Tito. Tito was a strong and decisive president, swiftly moving to rebuild his nation and putting the political and economic model of Communism into effect. But in his quest for stability, he employed methods that were often restrictive, and unrest stirred in the nation. After his death in 1980, his fellow Communist Slobodan Milosevic came to power and soon imposed even harsher policies on the Yugoslav people. Within a decade, war erupted, Yugoslavia splintered, and the new Serbia and Montenegro emerged.

Serbia and Montenegro

HUNGARY

ROMANIA

CROATIA

Subotica

Vojvodina

Tisza River

Novi Sad

Danube River

Beocin

Sava River

Belgrade

Sava River

Drina River

Danube River

BOSNIA-HERZEGOVINA

Golubac Castle

Majdanpek

Rudna Glava

Lazarevac

Valjevo

Serbia

Velika Morava River

Bajina Basta

Jagodina

Zapadna Morava River

Guca

Belgrade-Bar Railway

Stalac

Drina River

B   A   L   K   A   N   S

Juzna Morava River

Danube River

BULGARIA

Novi Pazar

Nis

Tara River

Piva River

Montenegro

Niksic

Kosovo Polje

Pristina

CROATIA

Crkvice

Podgorica

Kosovo and Metohija

Lipljan

Herceg Novi

Kotor

Cetinje

Debelde

Lake Scutari

Prizren

Bar

Adriatic Sea

ALBANIA

MACEDONIA

Legend

International border
Internal border
☆ Capital city
• City
■ Point of interest

0   50 Miles
0   50 KM

N

ATLANTIC OCEAN

RUSSIA

EUROPE

SERBIA AND MONTENEGRO

Black Sea

AFRICA

Mediterranean Sea

0   500 Miles
0   500 KM

Throughout all of this turmoil, a proud tradition of independence and resistance to conquest remained among the people of Serbia and Montenegro. Despite the many obstacles, their rich culture thrived over the years. Indeed, the story of Serbia and Montenegro has all the elements of an epic poem, a literary form dearly loved by the peoples of the region. Bitter tragedy, beloved heroes, and a fiery, unquenchable spirit—all set against a ruggedly beautiful landscape—make up this exciting but often sorrowful tale. In many ways, it is a story with many beginnings—of rebuilding and renewing over and over again.

Such rebuilding and renewal continues. The war crimes trial of Slobodan Milosevic revisited painful memories of his rule, only to be left unresolved when Milosevic died in March 2006. And greater changes began in May 2006, when Montenegrins voted for their republic to become independent from Serbia. Looking to the future, predicting the twists of fate that lie ahead for Serbia and Montenegro is difficult. The road to full separation for Montenegro will likely be long and challenging. In addition, with Kosovo's stability also an unresolved question, many uncertainties remain in that long-troubled region. Kosovo, too, is in the process of moving toward independence, although Serbia strongly resists any such change. Yet regardless of what the future holds, history shows that Serbia and Montenegro's people have the resilience and the resources to persevere.

Follow political developments resulting from Montenegro's and Kosovo's independence movements. Go to www.vgsbooks.com for links.

ALPHABET SOUP

When reading about Serbia and Montenegro in different sources, you might notice special marks over some letters. These marks are called diacritics. They represent letters in the Cyrillic alphabet (used by many Serbian and Montenegrin residents) that do not exist in the Roman alphabet. For ease of reading, this book does not include diacritics. Go to www.vgsbooks.com for links to learn more about languages and alphabets in Serbia and Montenegro.

THE LAND

The nation of Serbia and Montenegro lies on southeastern Europe's Balkan Peninsula, an outcropping of land that juts southward into the waters of the Mediterranean and Black seas. The nation is located on this wide peninsula's western edge, washed by an arm of the Mediterranean known as the Adriatic Sea.

With an area of 39,448 square miles (102,170 square kilometers), Serbia and Montenegro is slightly smaller than the state of Kentucky. While its land and water borders are relatively short at 1,519 miles (2,445 km) long, seven other countries border the nation. Several of these bordering countries are other former Yugoslav republics, including Bosnia-Herzegovina to the west, Croatia to the northwest, and Macedonia to the south. Among the non-Yugoslav nations that border Serbia and Montenegro is Albania, which also lies to the south. Romania and Bulgaria each share part of Serbia and Montenegro's eastern border, while Hungary is the nation's neighbor to the north.

▷ Topography

Three major regions define Serbia and Montenegro's landscape: Northern Plains, Central and Southern Mountains, and Southwestern Coastal Plains. These different areas give the nation a varied and beautiful landscape that visitors and locals have praised for hundreds of years.

Northern Serbia and Montenegro is made up mostly of broad, fertile plains. Part of southern Europe's Pannonian Plain (also called the Carpathian Basin), the region lay beneath a vast, shallow sea during the Pliocene Era that began about five million years ago. This body of water, known as the Pannonian Sea, left behind 2 to 2.5 miles (3.2 to 4 km) of sediment. This fertile soil makes the region a rich agricultural area.

Moving southward, the land rises to the Balkan Mountains, a range running southward from eastern Serbia. Within Serbia and Montenegro, many smaller ranges make up the Balkan range, including the Sar Planina and the Prokletije Mountains.

BLACK MOUNTAIN

Several theories exist regarding how Montenegro got its name, which comes from the Italian words for "black mountain." The name *Montenegro* first turned up in about 1276. It may have come from the dark forests of black pines that once blanketed Mount Lovcen in southwestern Montenegro. It also may have come from basalt—a black rock that makes up much of Mount Lovcen. Other historians have suggested that the name may come from Ivan Crnojevic, a fifteenth-century conqueror of lands that later became Montenegro—which is known to locals as Crna Gora.

To the west, roughly along the Montenegrin border, the Dinaric Alps run parallel to the Adriatic. Creating a dramatic boundary between the interior and the coastal plains, this range holds the nation's highest summit, Mount Daravica. This peak rises to 8,714 feet (2,656 meters) and straddles the border with Albania. The Dinaric range is also part of one of Serbia and Montenegro's most interesting features: its magnificent karst region. In the karst region, limestone formations—split primarily between the Dinaric Alps and the Balkans—are dotted with deep caves and shot through with underground rivers and lakes. Some of these vast caverns are open to the public and draw many visitors each year.

The Kopaonik massif is also in south-central Serbia and Montenegro. This long, wide granite ridge is made up of peaks reaching heights of more than 6,500 feet (1,981 m). This area is known for its natural beauty and diversity, as well as for its popular ski slopes. Serbia and Montenegro's mountainous beauty comes at a cost, however. The same ancient geologic activity that produced the nation's lovely landscape also created deep fault lines (cracks in the earth's crust) that sometimes cause severe earthquakes.

The final topographical region in Serbia and Montenegro lies to the west of the mountains, in Montenegro. A strip of land runs along the Adriatic Sea for about 125 miles (201 km), forming a narrow coastal plain. Much of this seaside region is rocky. But some stretches boast sand and pebble beaches that draw vacationers to Montenegrin shores.

◉ Rivers and Lakes

Serbia and Montenegro's most important river is the Danube, one of the great rivers of Europe. Flowing southward from Hungary, it traces Serbia's border with Croatia before turning eastward to cut across the northern portion of the country. It flows through Belgrade, the nation's capital city, and forms a stretch of the nation's boundary with Romania to the east. About 365 miles (588 km) of the Danube's total length is within Serbia and Montenegro's borders. The Sava, another major river in the north, flows into the country from the border with Bosnia-Herzegovina. The Sava joins the Danube in the heart of Belgrade. Most of Serbia and Montenegro's other rivers flow toward the basin formed by the Danube and the Sava. The Tisza is another major waterway. It waters the wide plains of the Vojvodina region. Sections of all these northern rivers can be navigated, making them valuable for transportation and business.

The Morava River is central and southern Serbia and Montenegro's main water route. The Morava begins as two branches, the Zapadna (West) Morava and the Juzna (South) Morava. The two come together at Stalac, a city in central Serbia. From there, the river flows northward to the Danube as the Velika Morava, or just the Morava. This centrally located river is short but wide enough to serve as a transportation route.

In the southwest, within Montenegro, the Piva and Tara rivers carve valleys through the mountains. They meet to form the Drina River, which in turn flows northward along Serbia's western border with Bosnia-Herzegovina before meeting the Sava.

Montenegro is the site of Lake Scutari (also known as Skadarsko Jezero). This freshwater lake lies on both sides of the Montenegrin-Albanian border. It is Serbia and Montenegro's largest lake, with an area that ranges between 150 and 205 square miles (389 and 531 sq. km), depending on seasonal rainfall. Bounded by mountains on two edges and plains on the other, the lake was once part of the Adriatic Sea.

The fourteenth-century Golubac Fortress overlooks the **Danube River.** Here the powerful river has cut a 2-mile-long (3.2 km) gorge through the Balkan Mountains. This corridor between dramatic cliffs is called the Iron Gate.

Climate

Most of western Montenegro's coastal region has a Mediterranean climate, with mild winters and hot, dry summers. The sirocco, a wind that blows across the Mediterranean Sea from Africa's Sahara, brings warm, moist air and winter rains.

On the other side of the Dinaric Alps, a continental climate takes hold. Seasons are more distinct. In particular, winters are colder. However, most of Montenegro remains pleasant. The city of Podgorica enjoys July temperatures of about 81°F (27°C) and cooler but still mild, winter temperatures around 43°F (6°C).

To the northeast, near the edge of the Pannonian Plain, Belgrade's averages are a bit lower. The city's summer temperatures hover around 71°F (22°C). Average winter temperatures fall to about freezing (32°F, or 0°C). The widest extremes between hot and cold are in the northern plains region, which is also exposed to the *kosava*, a bitterly cold seasonal wind. The icy kosava blows into Serbia from the northeast in the autumn and winter, whistling across the plains toward Belgrade. Throughout the country, mountainous areas have generally cooler temperatures year-round.

For some of the best weather in Serbia and Montenegro, many people head to Kopaonik—also known as Sunny Mountain—for its average of about two hundred sunny days per year.

Regional precipitation follows a similar pattern. Heavy snowfall blankets the mountains throughout the winter. However, the coastal region has the heaviest precipitation overall. The town of Crkvice, in the far western karst region, receives an average of nearly 200 inches (508 cm) of rain, compared to approximately 25 to 30 inches (64 to 76 cm) each year in Belgrade.

Flora and Fauna

Most of central Serbia and Montenegro was once richly forested, though many of its forests have been thinned over the years. Nevertheless, stands of deciduous (leaf-shedding) trees such as oak, elm, chestnut, ash,

Get a weather report and learn about the landscape, wildlife, and city life of Serbia and Montenegro. Visit www.vgsbooks.com for links.

and willow trees still blanket the land. At higher elevations, beech forests flourish. They eventually give way to deep evergreen forests of spruce and fir, which can survive at higher altitudes.

Once again, Montenegro's coastal climate is an exception. Palm trees and cypresses grow here, as well as fruit and nut-bearing trees such as fig, lemon, olive, and almond. Pomegranate bushes grow close to the earth, and local wine makers tend climbing grapevines. Overall, Serbia and Montenegro boasts one of the highest numbers of plant species of any country in Europe. Hundreds of species of flowering plants—from iris and lilac to violets and orchids—bloom on both the plains and the mountain slopes.

The nation is also home to a variety of animal life. Deer roam the country's forests and fields. The chamois—a small, goatlike member of the antelope family—clambers on mountain slopes. Wild boars are found in the north. Carnivorous mammals such as bears, wolves, lynxes, and pine martens (members of the weasel family) prey on hares, Dinaric voles (small, mouselike rodents), and other small mammals.

Serbia and Montenegro, despite its environmental setbacks and struggles, has a remarkable range of flora and fauna. The Sar Planina National Park is home to nearly 150 species of butterfly, as well as more than 200 bird species. Similarly, Lake Scutari boasts hundreds of species of fish, and Kopaonik supports 1,500 types of plants. In total, more than 40,000 species of flora and fauna have been identified in the region, making it a true environmental treasure.

Birds native to Serbia and Montenegro include quail, doves, partridges, and pheasants that live on the nation's plains. Marshy areas in the north are havens for wading herons and storks, while lakes support communities of waterfowl such as wild geese and ducks. In addition, the nation's lakes and rivers are home to a variety of fish, such as brown trout, carp, and eel. Along the Adriatic coastline, lobsters, shrimp, octopus, and many kinds of fish flourish.

Insect life is rich in Serbia and Montenegro as well. One of the most noteworthy insect inhabitants, making its home high on Mount Kopaonik, is the Siberian grasshopper. This unique species has wide, bulbous front legs that remind some observers of boxing gloves. In addition, more than eighty types of millipede live in Serbia and Montenegro, along with dozens of different moth species.

◐ Natural Resources and Environmental Challenges

Within its small area, Serbia and Montenegro contains a wealth of natural resources. Rich veins of valuable metals—including iron, copper, nickel, lead, and zinc—wind through the nation's mountains. The mountains also contain deposits of the precious metals gold and silver. Sources of fuel found within Serbia and Montenegro include oil and small reserves of natural gas. Still other natural resources are the nation's fertile agricultural land, its forests, and its many rivers.

However, Serbia and Montenegro also faces environmental problems. The wars that tore apart Yugoslavia in the early 1990s took a toll on the region's natural environment. Bombs introduced dangerous chemicals and devastated farmland and forest areas. Deforestation had already begun, and shortages of fuel, building materials, and other necessities during the war only made the problem worse. Deforestation, in turn, led to other problems such as soil erosion, a process by which valuable topsoil—unprotected by tree roots and forest cover—is washed away by rain and wind. Deforestation impacts the nation's wildlife as well, reducing the habitat of some animals.

Pollution is another issue confronting Serbia and Montenegro. Emissions from traffic and factories pollute large cities and industrial areas. Some of these factories have also released chemicals and other materials into the Sava River, which flows into the Danube.

The air over **Belgrade** is thick with automobile exhaust and other pollutants.

This pollution puts water wildlife—as well as people living along the riverbanks—at risk. The chemicals in fertilizers used on crops have also seeped into rivers and groundwater. In addition, the improper disposal of sewage has polluted the waters along the Adriatic coast.

The Serbian government has taken steps to address these problems. A national ministry devoted to the environment adopted a Serbian Law on Environmental Protection in 1991. In 2001 the nation also became a member of the Global Environment Facility (GEF). This organization helps countries start environmental protection programs. The government has introduced new laws setting limits on industrial waste and pollution. It has also started reforestation programs. In addition, several national parks and nature preserves are in place to protect the nation's wildlife.

Cities

BELGRADE was built at the meeting of the Danube and Sava rivers. Its residents enjoy breathtaking views. Historically, Belgrade's position was desirable for strategic reasons, and it has attracted settlers for as long as eight thousand years. The first to build major structures at the site were Celtic warriors. They constructed a fort at the meeting of the two rivers in the 200s B.C. Roman settlers followed in the first century B.C., and over the centuries, the city fell under the control of Byzantines, Huns, Ostrogoths, and other rulers. The Slavic ancestors of modern Serbs first came to the area in about the seventh century A.D. They gave the city its name—originally Beograd—in the 800s.

The name *Belgrade* means "white fortress" or "white town" in most regional languages. This name probably refers to the limestone walls that once surrounded the city.

Belgrade first became the capital of Serbia for a short period in the early 1400s. It became the capital of Yugoslavia in 1918 and of Serbia and Montenegro in 2003. With a present-day population of more than 1.1 million people, Belgrade is by far the nation's largest city. It is also a hub of cultural and commercial activity, with crowds of theatergoers and art lovers sharing the bustling streets with businesspeople and tourists.

PRISTINA, in the south-central region, is the nation's second-largest city. Pristina's population is difficult to estimate because of a large refugee population, but current guesses place the population as high as 500,000. It serves as the capital of the region known as Kosovo and Metohija (usually just called Kosovo).

The name *Novi Sad* can be translated "new field." Founded in 1694, the city is young by European standards.

NOVI SAD, lying on the Danube northwest of Belgrade, has about 190,000 people. As the capital of the Vojvodina region, it is also the main industrial center of the north, although its large oil refinery and other factories were badly damaged during the war.

PODGORICA is Montenegro's historical capital and still serves as that region's main governmental and cultural center, as well as the home of Serbia and Montenegro's justice system. The city was also Serbia's capital for a time during the 1000s, when it was known by the name of Ribnica. Modern Podgorica—whose name means "under the little mount," referring to its site at the base of a hill—is also Montenegro's largest city, with close to 150,000 residents.

SECONDARY CITIES Subotica is another significant town in Vojvodina, Serbia. Other important Montenegrin cities include Niksic and Cetinje, along with the Adriatic ports of Herceg Novi, Bar, and Kotor. Other important centers in south-central Serbia are Novi Pazar and Nis.

HISTORY AND GOVERNMENT

The earliest residents of the area that became Serbia and Montenegro are believed to have lived in caves on the Balkan Peninsula as long as forty thousand years ago. However, the first well-documented group was the Starcevo. These settlers appeared on the Danube's banks in about 6000 B.C. They were part of a society that extended over a large area of the Balkan Peninsula. The first Starcevo people probably lived by fishing, hunting, and gathering but went on to develop agriculture. Starcevo farmers raised crops of wheat, millet, and barley, and tended herds of cattle.

The Vinca society followed the Starcevo settlers. Named for its central village near modern Belgrade, this civilization emerged between 5000 and 4000 B.C. Some Vinca communities may have mined copper more than six thousand years ago, making them one of the first cultures known to do so.

A succession of other groups followed. During the 200s B.C, the Celts, originating in the present-day British Isles, formed a settlement

at the future site of Belgrade. The Roman Empire (a great civilization centered in Rome, Italy) drove them out in the first and second centuries A.D. The Romans built roads, bridges, theaters, and palaces throughout the Balkans.

In A.D. 395, the Roman Empire split into two parts. The region that would become Serbia and Montenegro fell into the Eastern, or Byzantine, Empire. This realm weakened during the fifth and sixth centuries A.D., as Byzantine rulers weren't able to defend against waves of attacks by invaders from the north. These attackers included Goths, Avars, and Slavs.

Slavic Settlement

The Slavs were a broad group made up of eastern European peoples who shared a common family of languages. The Serbs were one such Slavic group. Early in the 600s, they settled in the region that would become Serbia and Montenegro.

Early Serb communities were organized around extended family groups each known as a *zadruga*. Generally, several zadruge came under the authority of a leader called a *zupan*. Sometimes several of these zupani were governed by a *veliki zupan*, or grand zupan, similar to a prince.

Despite growing power, the Slavs' first centuries in the Balkans were times of turmoil. A zadruga and a zupan sometimes fought each other for control. In addition, the Serbs frequently had to defend their land. In the early 800s, a central Asian people called the Bulgars attacked Serbian villages. The Serbian prince Vlastimir realized that the Serbs would never be able to fight the Bulgars alone. He turned back to the Byzantine Empire, agreeing to accept its broad control in return for military help.

Prince Vlastimir's deal with the Byzantine Empire would have far-reaching results. One of the most significant was that Christianity—the official religion of the Byzantine Empire—was widely introduced to and accepted by the Serbian people. By the end of the ninth century, many had adopted the faith. After the Christian church split in 1054, Serbian Christians eventually joined the Eastern, or Orthodox, branch of Christianity.

▷ Princes, Kings, and Sultans

In 1169 Prince Stefan Nemanja took power. A skilled leader, he expanded Serbian territory, loosened Byzantine control, and established the powerful Nemanjic dynasty (family of rulers). In about 1196, his son took over the throne. In 1217 this son became Serbia's first king, taking the name Stefan Prvovencani, meaning "first-crowned." Two years later, Prvovencani's brother Sava helped start the independent Serbian Orthodox Church, part of Eastern Orthodoxy (a branch of Catholicism).

A series of Nemanjic kings followed. Daily life for many Serbs improved as agriculture and trades developed. In 1349 King Stefan Dusan took power and soon proved to be one of Serbia's greatest leaders. He introduced Dusan's Code, a set of laws defining proper behavior in everything from Christian worship to the use of grazing land. Dusan was also a brilliant military commander. He fought off internal revolts and outside attacks, and finally freed Serbia from the Byzantine Empire.

Throughout the mid-1300s, forces of the Ottoman Empire (a large realm centered in modern-day Turkey) began invading and seizing Serbian lands. The most famous battle came in June 1389, when Serbian prince Lazar Hrebeljanovic led an army against a large Ottoman force at the

Many fighters on both sides died in the June 1389 Battle of Kosovo Polje.

southern city of Kosovo Polje. Lazar was killed in the battle, as was the Ottoman leader, Sultan Murad I. While both sides suffered heavy losses, the Ottomans were ultimately victorious. Serbia's remaining holdings fell over the following decades. By the mid-1400s, the Ottoman Empire had claimed most of Serbia and its surrounding areas. Montenegro, with its hard-to-reach terrain, remained free of Turkish control.

Ottoman Rule

The Serbian struggle against the Ottomans was a battle for land and power. But Serbia's loss also had religious and cultural consequences. While the Serbs and most other Balkan groups were Christians, the Ottomans were followers of Islam, a religion founded on the Arabian Peninsula in the A.D. 600s. As the Ottoman Empire expanded, its leaders permitted the peoples of its vast new territories to continue practicing their own religions. However, Muslims (followers of Islam) had greater rights, so some people chose to convert—especially in the southern Kosovo region. For Christian families, the most troubling new Ottoman policy was *devshirme*. In this practice, the Ottomans took some Christian boys in each region from their homes and moved them to the Ottoman capital in Constantinople (present-day Istanbul, Turkey). There the boys were converted to Islam. Most of these boys were raised with fine food and clothing and excellent education, and some gained positions of power as adults. Nevertheless, Ottoman subjects hated devshirme.

As internal revolts and outside attacks weakened Ottoman control beginning in the late 1600s, high-ranking Ottoman soldiers called janissaries took matters into their own hands. They assassinated public officials who defied them, demanded extremely high taxes from the peasants, and robbed homes. Chaos in the countryside grew, and many common people lived in fear.

BLACK GEORGE

The revolt led by George Petrovic—a former pig trader also known as Karageorge, or Black George—raged for nearly ten years. The rebels faced huge odds. A ragtag force of farmer-soldiers, they were up against a much larger, better-armed, and better-trained Turkish military. The revolutionary force received some aid from Russia (then entangled in a conflict of its own with the Ottomans) and even managed to seize Belgrade. In the end, it wasn't enough, and the Ottomans finally triumphed. But Karageorge himself became a legend, and his descendants were important leaders in Serbia.

○ An Empire in Decline

By the early 1800s, the once-mighty Ottoman Empire was barely limping along. For Serbs a turning point came in 1804, when a revolutionary named George Petrovic led an uprising from a town near Belgrade. Although the Ottomans eventually defeated the rebels, the 1812 Treaty of Bucharest granted limited increases in Serbian freedom.

A more critical blow to Ottoman control came with another major revolt in 1815, led by Milos Obrenovic. In 1817 the uprising ended with the sultan agreeing to limited Serbian independence, though the territory would remain a Turkish possession. By 1830 the Serbs had gained full self-government, the Serbian Orthodox Church was granted independence, Ottoman forces were withdrawing, and Serbia was ruled by the newly crowned Prince Milos Obrenovic.

Obrenovic made many improvements to his realm. But he was a harsh ruler. Revolts soon pushed him from the throne and the country. His son took power briefly, followed by Alexander, the son of George Petrovic (also known as Karageorge). But Alexander's control slipped as Austria—a powerful nation to the north—sought to gain influence over Serbia. When Alexander was removed from the throne in 1858, the Obrenovics returned to rule.

The Obrenovic dynasty brought more changes to the country. In 1869 the government approved a constitution that gave greater power to the *skupstina* (a parliament, or lawmaking assembly). The constitution also increased civil rights for the Serbian people. These changes marked important steps toward a more democratic modern Serbia.

In 1875, during the reign of Milan Obrenovic II, new war erupted between the Ottomans and forces from Bosnia and Herzegovina. Serbia and its neighbor Montenegro joined the fight against the Ottomans, as did Russia. The 1878 Treaty of Berlin that ended the war awarded new territory to Serbia, while also taking some away. Montenegro gained the

Adriatic port of Bar. Most important, the treaty finally declared both Serbia and Montenegro independent of the Ottoman Empire.

Four years later, Milan named Serbia a kingdom and himself king. But internal unrest shook the kingdom. Milan's son Alexander took over in 1889 but fared little better than his father. In 1903 Alexander's reign ended bloodily when political enemies murdered him, his queen, and several officials.

Hoping to begin fresh, the skupstina handed the throne to Peter Karageorge. Obrenovic rule was over.

The Balkan Wars

King Peter's rule brought reforms to the Serbian constitution, economy, educational system, and army. The king was fortunate to have Nicola Pasic—a strong and skilled politician—as his prime minister (the skupstina's highest post). But the prosperity of his rule was short-lived. The first Balkan War erupted in October 1912, pitting the recently formed Balkan League—made up of Serbia, Montenegro, Greece, and Bulgaria—against the Ottomans. Supported by Russia, the Balkan League hoped to seize Macedonia and Kosovo, still held by the Ottoman Empire. By May 1913, the Balkan forces had—to the surprise of most observers—crushed the Ottomans. But just one month later, Bulgaria attacked Serbia over the way the captured lands had been distributed. Romania joined the fight against Bulgaria, as did Greece and the Ottomans. Bulgaria was swiftly defeated, and the Treaty of Bucharest ended the war in August 1913.

During the Balkan Wars, control of a route to the Adriatic Sea was one of the prizes most sought after by many in landlocked Serbia. In the First Balkan War, Serbia and Montenegro captured Albanian territory on the Adriatic coast. But many European nations were worried about Serbian power. They stepped in to create a new, larger, independent Albania, effectively preventing Serbia's expansion to the Adriatic.

In the end, the wars left tens of thousands dead and hundreds of thousands homeless. Refugee camps overflowed, and much of the country had been reduced to rubble.

The Great War

In 1914, as Serbia struggled to recover from the Balkan Wars, an event that would have far-reaching consequences took place nearly on the country's border. On June 28, Franz Ferdinand, the Archduke of Austria-Hungary, was assassinated during a visit to Sarajevo in Bosnia and Herzegovina. The archduke (heir to the Austrian throne) was assassinated by Gavrilo Princip, a Bosnian member of the Serbian group Union or Death, also known as the Black Hand. This secret organization opposed Austro-Hungarian interference in the Balkans.

Ferdinand's murder sparked international tensions that had been building for years. In the wake of the assassination, Austria-Hungary presented Serbia with an ultimatum demanding—among other things—permission for Austria-Hungary to send police into the country. Serbia did not agree to the terms, so Austria-Hungary declared war on July 28. Other nations followed quickly. Russia supported Serbia, while Germany sided with Austria-Hungary. Battle lines were soon drawn across Europe.

World War I—often called the Great War—was the largest in modern history. It pitted Germany, Austria-Hungary, Bulgaria, and the Ottoman Empire (known collectively as the Central powers) against Russia, Great Britain, France, Italy, Serbia, the United States, and Japan (called the Allies). Austro-Hungarian forces invaded Serbia in mid-August, and in the first months of the war, Serbia's army fought impressively, driving back a series of attacks. But it was not enough. In October 1915, Austria-Hungary, Germany, and Bulgaria made a fierce assault on Allied forces in Serbia. Before the end of the year, Serbia had fallen to the Central powers, its army shattered. Thousands of Serbian soldiers and civilians, desperate to escape the

During World War I, Serbians retreat from Austrian and Bulgarian armies.

advancing enemy, tried to flee into Montenegro and Albania. But the cruel winter journey through the western mountains killed many. In January 1916, Montenegro was captured as well.

As the war dragged on, Serbian forces regrouped and joined other Allied troops gathering in Macedonia. By September 1916, Serbian soldiers were back in action and began reclaiming enemy-held territory. In 1917 the Allies finally started gaining ground overall.

Birth of Yugoslavia

As the war's tide turned against the Central powers, exiled leaders from Serbia and its neighbors worked toward a bold new idea: a union of South Slavs, or Yugoslavs, including Serbs, Croats, and Slovenes. With this goal in mind, a Yugoslav Committee signed the Declaration of Corfu on July 20, 1917. This agreement laid the groundwork for the future Yugoslavia.

Meanwhile, the Allies defeated the Central powers. On November 11, 1918, Germany and the Allies signed a truce ending the war. The war's close saw two of Serbia's old enemies, the Ottoman Empire and Austria-Hungary, finally dissolve.

Even as these kingdoms broke apart, the new Kingdom of Serbs, Croats, and Slovenes was proclaimed on December 1, 1918. An elderly Peter Karageorge was formally given the grand title of King of the Serbs, Croats, and Slovenes, although the government's real power rested in the skupstina.

The new nation's leaders had plenty of work to do. Serbian forces alone suffered more than 330,000 casualties (dead, wounded, and taken prisoner)—nearly half the total number of its troops. Waves of typhus fever had swept through the country in 1915, killing hundreds of thousands. The land lay in ruins, with Belgrade virtually destroyed, and the war had left all of Europe deeply in debt.

Furthermore, control over the Kosovo region soon became a hotly debated issue. The territory had been under Serbian control since 1912, but its large ethnic Albanian population—mostly Muslim—wanted to become independent. Most Serbs felt fiercely attached to Kosovo. As the site of the fateful 1389 battle, Kosovo was widely viewed as the symbolic heart of Serbian history and ethnicity.

Meanwhile, Macedonians were unhappy with pressure to conform to Serbian culture. While the kingdom's different groups had much in common, old ethnic rivalries ran deep. Serbs were the largest single ethnicity, and other groups resented their influence in the new government. The kingdom's first constitution, adopted in 1921, only strengthened those feelings by essentially ignoring the realm's ethnic diversity.

The situation grew worse in June 1928 when a Montenegrin man opened fire during a skupstina session, killing three Croatian members. The resulting outrage threatened to plunge the nation into chaos. In early 1929, King Alexander (Peter Karageorge's son) desperately resorted to absolute rule, abolishing the constitution, dissolving the skupstina, and declaring himself dictator. He renamed the country Yugoslavia and divided it into nine provinces.

Although Alexander's drastic measures did force some stability upon Yugoslavia, unrest still simmered. Even after he loosened the reins slightly with another constitution in 1931, trouble continued to brew. In October 1934, Alexander was killed by an assassin believed to have ties to Croatia, Macedonia, and Bulgaria—all of which had complaints about his rule.

Alexander's only son, eleven-year-old Peter, was too young to take the throne. Alexander's cousin took over until 1935, when Milan Stojadinovic was named prime minister. Stojadinovic was an experienced politician, but his views soon brought trouble to Yugoslavia. He had made connections within Germany's Nazi Party, which had taken control two years earlier under the leadership of Adolf Hitler. The party

The assassination of King Alexander I in 1934 was the first to be captured in moving footage. At the time (before television), newsreels were often shown in movie theaters. The assassination was shown in movie theaters across Europe.

had many followers in Europe, but its tenets of racism and anti-Semitism (discrimination and hostility against Jews) troubled many others. So did its ties to Fascism, a repressive political system that dominated Italy under dictator Benito Mussolini. Still, Stojadinovic saw value in siding with Hitler and Mussolini, both of whom held tremendous power and sought still more. Stojadinovic met with them, founded Fascist organizations at home, and took the title Vodja (leader). When Dragisa Cvetkovic took over as prime minister in 1939, he continued along the same path.

> Would you like to learn more about the dramatic history of Serbia and Montenegro? Go to www.vgsbooks.com for links.

World War II and the Rise of Tito

On September 1, 1939, Germany invaded Poland and World War II began. Germany, Italy, and Japan joined to form the Axis powers. They fought the Allies, which included France, Britain, China, the Soviet Union (formerly Russia and other nations), and the United States.

On March 25, 1941, Serbia's Prince Paul signed the Axis Tripartite Pact with the Axis powers, agreeing to support them. But many Yugoslavs fiercely disagreed with the decision. The reaction was swift. Just two days later, with British help, Yugoslav military officers overthrew Paul's government and placed Alexander's son Peter—who was then eighteen years old—on the throne. Peter II quickly declared the nation neutral in the war.

However, it was too late to keep the conflict from Yugoslavia. Germany attacked on April 6. Its air force bombarded Belgrade for days. Much of the army deserted (left without permission), and Yugoslavia fell eleven days later. The Axis powers divided its territory among themselves. They set up new governments that were largely powerless.

Resistance to the occupation was fierce, especially in the land's rugged mountainous regions. One resistance group was the Chetniks, a mostly Serbian band of fighters. Another was the Yugoslav National Liberation Army, headed by a Croatian worker named Josip Broz, known as Tito. Also called the Partisans, Tito's resistance force was one of the largest and best organized. Founded on Communism (a political and economic theory based on ideas of shared property and social equality), the Partisans attracted many non-Serbs.

The practice of targeting and killing a group of people based on their ethnicity is called genocide or ethnic cleansing. It would be World War II's most terrible legacy. Hitler conducted mass genocide against Europe's Jews, killing a total of six million in the Holocaust. Some Serbs were guilty of helping Nazi forces capture, imprison, and execute Serbian Jews, while some Chetniks carried out attacks on Muslims. Members of a Croatian group called the Ustase targeted non-Croat and non-Catholic civilians.

As the war raged on, Tito emerged as a strong figure, and his group gained the support of the Allies. By 1944 he had begun to plan for a post-war government—of which he would be the head. When the war finally ended in May 1945, Tito was the clear leader of the new Yugoslavia.

MIDDLE MAN

In the years following World War II, a conflict known as the Cold War (1945–1991) developed. This "war" was not one of outright combat. It was a period of intense competition and suspicion between Communist and noncommunist nations, especially the Soviet Union and the United States. At the time, the Soviet Union—led by dictator Joseph Stalin—had a powerful influence and a tight hold over most of Europe's Communist nations. But Tito defied Stalin, refusing to let the Soviet Union control Yugoslavia. This stance led to bitter hostility between Stalin and Tito but also allowed Communist Yugoslavia to remain on friendly terms with noncommunist nations. This unique position in the middle gave Yugoslavia greater independence than other Communist countries during the Cold War.

◎ Communist Years

Yugoslavia had lost at least one million people in the war, and Belgrade had been flattened once more. For the second time in thirty years, the nation faced the task of rebuilding.

Tito set about forming a Communist government. He renamed the nation the Federal People's Republic of Yugoslavia (FNRJ), introduced a new constitution, and held elections for a national assembly.

Tito pictured the new Yugoslavia as a federation of Serbia, Montenegro, Croatia, Slovenia, Macedonia, and Bosnia-Herzegovina. Two autonomous (self-governing) regions, Kosovo and Vojvodina, were also established. Although some Serbs felt cheated by the change, it was popular among other groups. Tito modeled Yugoslavia's Communist system after that of the Soviet Union. However, over the next decade, his approach evolved into a unique brand of Communism—sometimes called Titoism.

Yugoslavia's postwar recovery progressed quickly at first. Industry and agriculture thrived. But by the 1960s, some Yugoslavs opposed Communist policies including media censorship, the ban on other political parties, and harsh treatment of religious institutions. In June 1968, antigovernment protests broke out in Belgrade as students took to the city's streets. Meanwhile, ethnic divisions reemerged. In November 1968, Kosovo erupted into riots as the region's large Albanian minority demanded greater rights. Macedonia saw similar protests in 1968, and Croatia had the Croatian Spring of 1971, when antigovernment demonstrations and publications called for greater rights in the republic.

Tito

Tito introduced a new constitution in 1974. It increased some freedoms for the Yugoslav republics, provinces, and people. Tito also hoped it would hold the country together after his death. To accomplish this goal, the constitution increased the president's power, reinforced Communism, and established a collective presidency in which a rotating group of leaders would take Tito's place. On May 4, 1980, Tito died. Whatever his faults and his mistakes, he had been a strong leader who had unified Yugoslavia for more than three decades.

Change from Within

Following Tito's death, the collective presidency took over the federal Yugoslavian government, and regional leaders continued to govern the republics. But cracks soon appeared in the system, and they started in Kosovo. In March 1981, Albanians there staged protests that began peacefully but grew violent. Yugoslavian police stopped the riots, which were followed by thousands of arrests, an increased police presence in Kosovo, and many violations of the population's civil rights. The turmoil drove thousands of families to leave their homes.

A brief bright spot came in 1984 when Bosnia and Herzegovina's capital, Sarajevo, hosted the Winter Olympics. The games brought both much-needed income and positive attention. Political scandals were everywhere. Ethnic tensions had been dangerously reignited, especially between Serbs and Albanians living in Kosovo.

Amid this chaos, a relatively little-known politician emerged as a powerful force. Slobodan Milosevic, the head of the Serbian Communist Party, gained support from both Serbs and Montenegrins throughout the late 1980s. In 1989 he was elected president of the Serbian Republic.

Milosevic believed in Serbian nationalism (fierce loyalty to one's own nation). With such a strongly pro-Serb president in office in Serbia and his supporters in control of three other Yugoslav governments, many non-Serbs felt an urgent need for independence. Demonstrations and strikes spread across the country, and Milosevic ordered troops to stop such activities. Meanwhile, other Communist regimes throughout Europe were crumbling.

Determined to create a state that housed the majority of Serbs within its borders, Milosevic vowed to seize all Serbian lands from any republic that seceded (separated) from Yugoslavia. But nothing he did could keep the country together. In 1991 Slovenia and Croatia declared independence, followed by Bosnia-Herzegovina and Macedonia in 1992.

Slovenia and Macedonia seceded with relatively little fighting, but Croatia erupted into war between ethnic Croats and Serbs. As fighting continued there, internal rivalries among Serbs, Croats, and Muslims in Bosnia-Herzegovina also heated up.

Meanwhile, officials at the highest levels of Yugoslavia's central government began resigning, stating that the unified Yugoslav nation had disappeared. In April 1992, a new Federal Republic of Yugoslavia was created, comprised of Serbia and Montenegro, including Kosovo and Vojvodina.

As foreign governments formally recognized the independence of these new nations, Milosevic and Serbia continued to resist the tide of change. Milosevic supported the Serbs fighting in both Croatia and Bosnia-Herzegovina. He ordered troops of the Army of Yugoslavia—made up of Serbs—to intervene. In March 1993, Bosnia exploded into full-fledged war.

During the Bosnian war, thousands of non-Serbs were imprisoned in hard-labor camps or killed in waves of ethnic cleansing. These events caused many to recall the horror of World War II. Smaller numbers of Serbs were also targeted and killed. Milosevic—who had steadily tightened his hold on Serbia and Montenegro even as other republics slipped from his grasp—was accused of supporting the worst of the violence. As punishment for his actions, outside nations placed a series of sanctions and embargoes (economic restrictions) on the new Yugoslavia.

Meanwhile, representatives of the United Nations (or UN—an international organization formed after World War II to work for peace) negotiated a series of unsuccessful cease-fires. The international military alliance North Atlantic Treaty Organization (NATO) also worked toward making peace.

As war raged all around Serbia, Serbs at home faced huge inflation (rapidly rising prices) and rising unemployment. Refugees streamed into the country, fleeing war zones in other Yugoslav republics. Then, in November 1994, Serbia itself came under NATO air strikes as retaliation for its actions in Bosnia. As international pressure on Milosevic increased, he finally agreed to negotiate. In the winter of 1995, leaders of the different ethnic groups signed peace accords that ended the war in Bosnia. An estimated 200,000 or more people were dead, thousands of others had been imprisoned, tortured, and raped, and about 2 million were homeless.

● Ongoing Struggles

The horror of the war had left Milosevic unpopular at home and abroad. Skupstina elections in November 1996 clearly showed his loss of support when an opposition party won seats in many parts of Yugoslavia. Milosevic declared the election results invalid, sparking protests around the country. Although measures against the protesters were harsh, the demonstrations lasted into February 1997 and finally convinced the government to accept the election. The victory ultimately had little impact, however, as the newly elected officials agreed on few issues other than their opposition to Milosevic. In fact, in July 1997, Milosevic claimed the post of president of all Yugoslavia for himself, increasing his power even more.

New trouble also came to Kosovo. An ethnic Albanian force called the Kosovo Liberation Army (KLA) had begun attacking Serbian police officers. The KLA drove Serbs from their homes and used other surprise attacks to fight for its goal of an independent Kosovo. In February 1998, Milosevic responded by ordering Yugoslavian troops into Kosovo to crush the KLA. When Milosevic's forces killed dozens of Albanians, including women and children, riots erupted in Pristina. With violence escalating rapidly, NATO intervened once again. When Milosevic rejected peace treaties, NATO forces began bombing Yugoslavia in March 1999. The strikes were devastating to both the military and the

A NATO bomb damaged this **Ministry of Defense building** in Belgrade in 1999.

Grim-faced **ethnic Albanian refugees** crowd onto the back of a truck to get out of Kosovo. They are fleeing from advancing Serbian troops in May 1999.

civilian populations. Meanwhile, Yugoslavia's Serbian forces attacked ethnic Albanians in another campaign of ethnic cleansing. They killed thousands of people and forced more than a million more out of their homes.

Faced with overwhelming international criticism, Milosevic agreed to peace talks in May. The bombing ended in early June, and approximately fifty thousand foreign troops led by NATO were stationed in Kosovo to keep the peace. Once again, Yugoslavia was struggling to cope with thousands of deaths, hundreds of thousands of refugees, and a landscape and economy devastated by bombing.

Milosevic also faced consequences of the Kosovo conflict. The International Criminal Tribunal for the former Yugoslavia (ICTY) charged him with committing war crimes. In September 2000 presidential elections, Milosevic lost to opposition leader Vojislav Kostunica. Milosevic tried to declare the results invalid and call for another election. But Serbs—most of them eager to be rid of him—finally forced him to step down in October. After eleven years, Yugoslavia had a new leader.

Kostunica had a huge task in rebuilding Yugoslavia. Kosovo had new leadership of its own under President Ibrahim Rugova— Kosovo's first democratically elected president. However, violence still flared in the region occasionally, and it was still under the control

Slobodan Milosevic

of the UN Interim Administration Mission in Kosovo (UNMIK).

Toward a New Union

Montenegro's status still remained a question. Although relations between Serbia and Montenegro were relatively calm, tension did exist. And as the only former Yugoslav republic other than Serbia that had not yet claimed independence, it seemed likely that Montenegro might still attempt to secede.

In 2002 the Serbian and Montenegrin governments took a step toward such independence. Plans were made to dissolve the Federal Republic of Yugoslavia and create Serbia and Montenegro in its place. This new union was designed as a loosely joined federation of two equal republics. Kosovo would remain under the watch of international organizations but was once again granted a measure of self-rule within Serbia, as was Vojvodina.

In February 2003, a new constitution made the creation of Serbia and Montenegro official. Svetozvar Marovic was elected president of the union in March. That same month, Serbia's popular prime minister, Zoran Djindjic, was assassinated. His killer was believed to be part of an organized crime group, and a massive crackdown on such organizations followed, leading to thousands of arrests. In addition, Montenegro finally elected Filip Vujanovic president in May. And in March 2004, Serbia—still lacking an elected president—named Kostunica as prime minister.

TRIAL OF THE CENTURY

In February 2002, all eyes turned to Milosevic's trial at the UN war crimes tribunal (an international court set up specifically to try cases involving war crimes). Always a controversial figure, Milosevic maintained that reputation in court from the beginning of the trial. He was charged with more than sixty war crimes, including "calculated cruelty." Despite facing vivid testimony by close to three hundred witnesses, Milosevic continued to insist upon his own innocence with fiery speeches. The intensely fought trial was still dragging on in September 2005, more than three years after it began. Throughout the proceedings, Milosevic continued to affirm his innocence. The trial plodded on for years before ending abruptly in March 2006, when Milosevic died of a heart attack. His defenders claimed that he had been mistreated in prison and denied medical care. At the time of his death, only about fifty hours of testimony remained in the trial. While many were not sad to see him go, tens of thousands honored him at a farewell ceremony in Belgrade.

Soon afterward, serious clashes erupted in Kosovo, pitting Serbs and Albanians against one another in the worst violence since 1999. NATO provided additional troops to stem the wave of fighting, and several thousand people fled from their homes in a bitter replay of past suffering.

In June 2004, Boris Tadic was elected president of Serbia, inspiring many Serbs to hope that political stability might finally be near. But leaders in both Serbia and Montenegro face enormous challenges in finding peace among their nations' ethnic groups, achieving strong and fair leadership, and securing basic rights for their people. Meanwhile, tensions periodically flare between the separate republics of Serbia and Montenegro. In February 2005, the Montenegrin president, Filip Vujanovic, spoke in favor of independence. The idea gained momentum in 2006, when Montenegrins debated the issue for a referendum. An estimated 86 percent of eligible Montenegrin voters cast their ballots on May 21, 2006. By a narrow margin, they chose to separate from Serbia. The vote was just the first in a series of steps toward full independence.

Boris Tadic

Kosovo also is moving toward independence, but Serbian resistance to this development remains very strong. International observers fear that, whatever the outcome for this area—which has been fought over so fiercely and for so long—it may spark new conflict. At the very least, Kosovo's independence could spur a massive migration of ethnic Serbs from the area, presenting new challenges for the former federation.

◉ Government

According to Serbia and Montenegro's February 2003 constitution, the union's central government is headed by a president and vice president, each of whom are elected by the national assembly and serve terms of four

Montenegro's independence vote, called a referendum, asked just one question: "Do you want the Republic of Montenegro to be an independent state with full international and legal subjectivity [status]?" Voters checked either yes or no. By an agreement signed between Serbia and Montenegro, 55 percent of Montenegrin voters needed to vote yes for independence. The final count placed the yes vote at about 55.4 percent. For links to the latest news about independence for Montenegro and Kosovo, go to www.vgsbooks.com.

Serbia and Montenegro's **national assembly** meets in this building in Belgrade.

years. To maintain a balance of power between the republics, the president and vice president may not both be from the same republic.

Legislative duties belong to the union's national assembly. Its 126 members—91 from Serbia and 35 from Montenegro—serve four-year terms. The assembly, in turn, elects judges to Serbia and Montenegro's court system. Judges are equally divided between Serbs and Montenegrins.

In addition to shared federal structures, Serbia and Montenegro each has its own constitution, president, and assembly. The republics have individual flags, anthems, and national currencies, as well. Kosovo and Metohija and Vojvodina remain officially autonomous provinces within Serbia.

If Montenegro follows through on the referendum vote, much of this will change. The shared federal structures will disappear, and Serbia and Montenegro will each have their own fully independent government.

THE PEOPLE

Serbia and Montenegro's 10.7 million people have seen more than their share of hard times. The war and turmoil of the late twentieth century rekindled old ethnic rivalries and set new tensions aflame. But even as this troubled nation struggles to overcome major obstacles, it draws upon its people's rich background and strong spirit to reach its goals.

Serbia and Montenegro has an average population density of 271 people per square mile (105 people per sq. km), compared to 197 people per square mile (76 people per sq. km) in neighboring Bosnia-Herzegovina and 79 people per square mile (31 people per sq. km) in the United States. However, because settlement is lighter in the rugged mountainous region that covers much of Serbia and Montenegro, the country's cities and plains are actually much more crowded than this figure suggests. More than half of Serbs and Montenegrins live in urban areas, and Belgrade alone is home to approximately 15 percent of the federation's people.

With an estimated annual growth rate of just 0.2 percent, Serbia and Montenegro's total population should remain about the same in coming

years. In fact, with Serbian and Montenegrin women having an average of 1.7 children in their lifetimes, the population is actually projected to drop as much as 4 percent by 2050.

However, these figures only reflect population growth based on births and deaths. They do not account for the migration of refugees driven from their homes by war, persecution, and unrest. In modern Serbian and Montenegrin history, hundreds of thousands of such people have traveled back and forth across national borders in search of safety. This movement causes dramatic shifts in population distribution, density, and other characteristics. In 1999, at the close of the Kosovo conflict, nearly one million people had come to Serbia and Montenegro as refugees and internally displaced people, or IDPs (people uprooted from their homes but still within the borders of their country). By 2004 those numbers—though still hard to pin down—had shrunk significantly. But thousands of refugees and IDPs remain in Serbia and Montenegro, presenting an ongoing challenge for social organizations.

PLIGHT OF THE ROMA

The Roma—often called Gypsies—are one of Serbia and Montenegro's many ethnic groups. Believed to have roots in India, the Roma left their ancient homeland hundreds of years ago and settled throughout Europe, Asia, and the Americas. As they have in many countries in Europe, the Roma have suffered severe and sometimes even violent discrimination in Serbia and Montenegro. With limited access to jobs, education, and other opportunities, most Roma are very poor. Many homeless families live in makeshift communities under bridges, in cemeteries, and at garbage dumps. Hoping to better the lives of Serbia and Montenegro's Roma, international organizations such as the United Nations are working to protect their rights.

◎ Ethnic Groups

Serbia and Montenegro's people are made up of a diverse range of ethnic groups. This mixture has frequently been the source of conflict, especially during the Yugoslav years. However, it also gives Serbia and Montenegro a uniquely rich and varied social landscape.

The majority of the federation's population—about 63 percent—is ethnically Serb. Due to the turmoil of recent years, this number (and many other demographic statistics) is difficult to pinpoint exactly, especially in turbulent Kosovo. Nevertheless, Serbs have long been the largest and most dominant group in the region, dating back to early South Slavic settlers more than one thousand years ago. And while most Serbs live in Serbia and Montenegro, they also make up significant populations in other Balkan and Eastern European nations. Serbs take great pride in their shared ethnicity. The Eastern Orthodoxy—especially the Serbian Orthodox Church—is a major unifying force. In addition, Serbs see the historical Battle of Kosovo Polje as a symbol of their strong spirit and fierce independence.

Montenegrins, also South Slavs and also members of Eastern Orthodoxy, are often described as "close cousins" to the Serbs. Historians disagree on exactly when, how, or even if Montenegrins became ethnically separate from Serbs. Nevertheless, Montenegrins have a distinct national identity from both Serbs and other groups in Serbia and Montenegro. They are the largest group within the republic of Montenegro, accounting for more than 60 percent of its population.

However, Montenegrins are actually only the third-largest overall, making up just 5 percent of Serbia and Montenegro's total population. Serbia and Montenegro is actually home to more ethnic Albanians than Montenegrins, with more than 16 percent of the population thought to be Albanian. This non-Slavic group differs culturally from the Slavs in important ways, particularly religion. Most Albanians are Muslims, while nearly all Serbs and Montenegrins are members of the Eastern Orthodox Church.

Serbia and Montenegro is also home to smaller communities of Croats, Hungarians, Slovaks, Macedonians, Romanians, Bulgarians, and other groups. Differences in language, religion, and history all distinguish these ethnic minorities from one another. While no single group has a large population, they collectively make up about 16 percent of the country's population.

Language

Serbia and Montenegro's complicated and war-torn past has left a patchwork of languages and alphabets in use within the nation's borders. The official language of unified Yugoslavia was Serbo-Croatian. In the federation of Serbia and Montenegro and in other parts of the former Yugoslavia, most people continue to speak dialects (regional variations) of Serbo-Croatian. But since Yugoslavia's disintegration, these dialects have come to be defined as much by who is speaking them as by the language itself. For example, the language spoken by Serbs is called Serbian, while Croats speak Croatian. However, these languages are extremely similar in grammar, vocabulary, and other main characteristics. The biggest difference between them is that Serbians use the Cyrillic script (an alphabet used by missionaries in the A.D. 800s to translate religious texts into Slavic languages), while Croatian is written with the Latin alphabet used in Western Europe and the Americas. Montenegrins speak Serbian but use both Cyrillic and Latin alphabets.

Due to variations in the language once known as Serbo-Croatian, multiple words often exist to describe the same things in Serbia and Montenegro. For example, the word for "milk" is *mleko* in Serbian but *mlijeko* in Croatian. Similarly, the Serbian translation of "world" is *svet*, while Croatian-speakers say *svijet*. However, there is also a great deal of overlap, and both Serbs and Croats call a window a *prozor*.

This street sign uses both Cyrillic script *(top)* and the Latin alphabet to identify the city of Novi Sad.

Albanians, on the other hand, speak a unique language. Albanian is not directly related to any other modern language. In addition, many Hungarians, Romanians, and other minorities within Serbia and Montenegro's borders speak their own languages.

Education

Education in Serbia and Montenegro has a long history. The earliest centers of learning were founded to teach religion around A.D. 1000. The church remained the main provider of education into the 1800s, with schools housed in monasteries and other religious institutions. One of the first major secular (nonreligious) educational institutions was the Great School, founded in 1808. The Great School later became the University of Belgrade.

In modern times, all Serbian and Montenegrin children are required to attend eight years of elementary education, beginning at the age of seven. Following graduation from primary school, students may choose to attend technical, vocational, art, or teaching schools, all of which provide training in specific

HE STARTED IT

Serbia and Montenegro's long tradition of education reaches back to the 1200s and Saint Sava, the founder of the Serbian Orthodox Church. In an effort to develop education among his people, Sava built schools and translated books into the local tongue. For these works, he is considered the patron (protector) saint of Serbian education. Schoolchildren across the federation celebrate his feast day on January 27.

Saint Sava

Children study hard in this **classroom in Debelde, a village in Kosovo.** To learn more about education and health issues in Serbia and Montenegro, go to www.vgsbooks.com for links.

trades and skills. Other students continue on to three or four years of secondary school. From there, they may choose one of Serbia and Montenegro's colleges or universities. In addition to the University of Belgrade, Podgorica hosts the campus of the University of Montenegro. Other major institutions are in Nis and Novi Sad.

An estimated 97 percent of children do attend the required years of elementary school. The nation's literacy rate is high, with approximately 98 percent of adults able to read and write. However, these numbers are lower in rural areas and in areas badly damaged by war. Kosovo's schools—especially those that once taught ethnic Albanians—suffered the most during the conflict. Many were destroyed, and rebuilding has been a long process. Among the refugee population, which has placed stress on the educational system, many children have not been able to attend school consistently or have had to leave altogether. And as displaced families struggle to survive, children may have to drop out and work to help their parents make ends meet.

◉ Health

Serbia and Montenegro's national health statistics offer clues to the nation's troubled recent history. While similar to numbers from surrounding countries, they tend to paint a dark picture of Serbian and Montenegrin health compared to most other European nations. For example, Serbia and Montenegro has an infant mortality rate of 13 deaths per 1,000 babies born, along with a maternal mortality rate—the number of women who die during childbirth or due to pregnancy-related complications—of 11 women per 100,000 births. Similarly, the average life expectancy is 73 years (70 for men and 75 for women). These numbers indicate problems in national health care. Although Serbian and Montenegrin citizens are guaranteed care under a federal medical insurance system, public hospitals and other medical facilities are often war-damaged and run-down, especially in rural areas. Supplies are frequently scarce, and those that are available are often of poor quality. A small number of private clinics also exist, but the treatment they offer isn't much better than the care available in public facilities.

In March 2006, health officials in western Serbia confirmed that several dead birds, including a domestic rooster, had been infected with avian influenza (bird flu). This virus is deadly to humans. To stop it from spreading to other birds and to humans who handle birds, thirty-two flocks of domestic poultry in the area were put down. Exports of poultry products were prohibited. However, the bigger concern is that the deadly virus may mutate into a form that can be passed from person to person. Officials in Serbia and Montenegro continue to monitor the situation closely.

Not surprisingly, many of Serbia and Montenegro's ongoing health concerns spring from the war. Ravaged by years of conflict, homes and villages across the country are still rebuilding, and living conditions are poor for many. This problem is especially great for refugees and IDPs, many of whom live in overcrowded camps. Access to proper sanitation, while quite high in urban areas, falls off in the countryside. In the camps, the situation is often worse, and diseases can spread quickly.

In addition, the war left behind the major problem—and health threat—of land mines. These weapons, which are usually half-buried in the ground, explode when weight is placed on them. A single person can be enough to activate a mine. The resulting blast—when not deadly—often results in the loss of one or more limbs. Such injuries create a significant health-care challenge for Serbia and Montenegro, which is one of the most heavily mined countries in Europe. In 2003 national officials signed the international Mine Ban Treaty, which outlaws the production and use of land mines. However, until remaining mines are removed from the land, they continue to pose a great danger.

Serbia and Montenegro may also face a future crisis with the deadly disease acquired immunodeficiency syndrome (AIDS), caused by the human immunodeficiency virus (HIV). An estimated 0.2 percent of the adult population is infected with HIV/AIDS. While this percentage is relatively low, it still translates to approximately 10,000 people living with the virus. And because AIDS education is limited, that number could rise. Health experts worry that should the nation's HIV/AIDS rate increase, Serbia and Montenegro's already overburdened health-care system would be unable to handle the demands of caring for AIDS patients.

BODY AND SOUL

One major health concern in Serbia and Montenegro is the mental and emotional strain caused by many years of turmoil. Psychological care is especially important for young adults who were children during the war. These people may have struggled with traumas such as the loss of a family member, a frightening escape from a family home, or simply witnessing violence and suffering. While such problems may not seem as urgent as other needs, caring for the mental health of Serbia and Montenegro's people is a long-term necessity.

Human Rights

The violation of human rights in Serbia and Montenegro is another challenge facing the federation's people and government. The constitution states the goals of "respect for human rights of all persons" and an aim "to preserve and promote human dignity, equality and the rule of law." Most observers agree that the overall human rights situation in the federation has improved dramatically since the 1990s. However, memories of the war's genocide are still fresh. Discrimination and violence based on ethnicity and religion are still reported throughout Serbia and Montenegro and the entire former Yugoslavia—especially in Kosovo.

Ongoing problems include police brutality, unjust arrests and imprisonment, and prejudice or violence against women and ethnic minorities. Women and children are also at risk of being trafficked, or smuggled, to other countries and forced into servitude or prostitution. Serbia and Montenegro is also believed to be a route used by traffickers between other countries.

CULTURAL LIFE

While Serbia and Montenegro's fractured history has caused deep unrest and hardship over the years, it has also given the nation a cultural life of great variety and range. From long-held religious beliefs and prized ancient literature to modern music and sporting events, this small nation contains a wealth of cultural treasure.

▷ Religion

For centuries, religion has been an important source of identity for many people in what became Serbia and Montenegro. Sometimes it has been a positive force, preserving traditions and offering hope and community in the face of war. However, it has also brought tragedy to the nation. Bitter prejudices have sometimes sparked conflict between groups. In particular, Serbian Orthodox Christians have clashed with Muslims.

However, long before either Christianity or Islam came to the region, early Slavs—including the ancestors of many residents of mod-

ern Serbia and Montenegro—shared an ancient belief system. Followers of this religion worshipped many deities (gods and goddesses), each representing certain aspects of the natural world. The faith was strong among the ancient Serbs, and traces of it remain in modern Serbian Orthodoxy.

The Byzantine Empire first brought Christianity to the Balkans as early as the fourth century A.D., but the religion found little foothold until the 800s. Islam followed around the beginning of the 1400s, introduced by the region's Ottoman conquerors. Both faiths gradually attracted a following among the local peoples.

During the Communist era in the twentieth century, religion faced a major setback. In general, Communist governments are atheist (nonreligious). They state that the people's main focus should be their country and fellow citizens rather than religion. Officially, Yugoslavia's Communist authorities did not encourage religious worship and specifically banned using the church for political purposes.

However, religion was not forbidden. Serbs and Montenegrins of all religions were, in theory, free to practice their faiths. But the government strictly monitored religious publications, teaching, and other church activities. As time went by, many people began practicing their religion in secret or abandoned it altogether.

In modern times, however, religion plays a growing role in the daily life of many Serbian and Montenegrin citizens. The vast majority of ethnic Serbs still belong to the Serbian Orthodox Church, as do most Montenegrins. In all, about 65 percent of the federation's people are Eastern Orthodox Christians. Most Christians in Serbia and Montenegro observe major holidays such as Easter (the celebration of Jesus' resurrection) and Christmas (the holiday marking the birth of Jesus). Orthodox services for these holidays are solemn but beautiful ceremonies. They are often followed by shared family feasts.

Many Orthodox Serbs observe a holiday called the Krsna Slava. This long-standing tradition—believed to be at least 1,200 years old—honors a family's patron saint. Many people view the Slava as a spiritual birthday. It commemorates the day on which the first member of the family converted to Christianity, and it is often celebrated in place of personal birthdays. The occasion is a time for prayer and remembrance, as well as for welcoming guests and sharing holiday meals.

Another 20 percent of the population identify themselves as Muslims. The nation's Islamic communities are primarily in the Kosovo region, as well as in the town of Novi Pazar in Serbia. For Muslims in Serbia and Montenegro, one of the most important religious events of the year is Ramadan, Islam's holy month. All Muslims fast (refrain from eating) from sunrise to sunset during Ramadan. At the end of the month, they celebrate with the festival of Eid al-Fitr. Other major Islamic holidays include Eid al-Adha, which falls during the hajj—the annual pilgrimage to Mecca, Saudi Arabia (Islam's holiest city). All Muslims try to make the hajj at least once. It takes place during the Islamic month of Dhu al-Hijjah, the last month of the Islamic calendar. This month falls between late November and January, depending on lunar cycles.

In addition to these main religious communities, smaller numbers of Serbian and Montenegrin citizens are Roman Catholic, Protestant, Jewish, atheist, or members of other faiths. Members of these other faiths total about 15 percent of the population.

Islamic communities all over the world worship in mosques. In Prizren, Kosovo, **Sinan Pasha Mosque** *(center)* was built on a hilltop in 1615. Its minaret (tower), which is 1,713 feet (43.5 m) in height, can be seen from great distances.

◉ Literature

Serbia and Montenegro's rich literary history has its beginnings in ancient oral traditions. Long before developments such as the printing press made it easy to preserve literature through books, storytellers passed tales, poetry, and songs down through the generations. Many of these stories were epic sagas of battles and bravery, while others told of tragic romances. Storytelling custom was especially important to the people of Serbia and Montenegro during times of occupation, such as the long period under the Ottomans. Even as outside rulers attempted to dominate local culture, the telling and retelling of stories kept the people's history and spirit alive.

After the A.D. 800s, Christianity became the main influence on Serbian literature and remained so throughout most of the Middle Ages (about A.D. 500–1500). At first, much of this writing simply chronicled current church and political events, often praising or denouncing one leader or another based on the church's opinions. However, around the end of the 1200s, a more creative type of writing emerged. A biography of Saint Sava by the monk Theodosius was especially notable for its vivid language.

In 1389 an even more imaginative and poetic style came about with numerous retellings of Prince Lazar's tragic death in the Battle of Kosovo Polje. Another major literary figure in the late 1300s was Marko Kraljevic. This beloved hero had, like Prince Lazar, fought against the Ottomans, as had his beloved horse, Sharats. Marko's fame was so great throughout the Balkans that he is also featured in the stories of Croatia, Albania, Bulgaria, and Macedonia.

In the 1700s and 1800s, some Serbian and Montenegrin writers looked to their nation's history for inspiration. Vuk Stefanovic Karadzic collected age-old stories, songs, and proverbs in book form. In 1754 Bishop Vasilije Petrovic published one of the first detailed histories of Montenegro. Petar Petrovic Njegos—nicknamed the Shakespeare of Montenegro—drew on regional history to compose *The Mountain Wreath*, a play in verse.

As time went on, new authors told tales in the everyday language of average people. Jakov Ignatovic was one of Serbia's first great novelists, writing in a modern, realistic style. Jovan Sterija Popovic used many of the same ideas in plays such as *The Patriots*. Prominent twentieth-century authors included Isidora Sekulic, who wrote short stories as well as novels and essays, and Milos Crnjanski, known for works such as the novel *Seobe* (Migrations) and the poem "Lament over Belgrade." Other contemporary Serbian and Montenegrin authors include Rastko Petrovic, Milorad Pavic, Danilo Kis, Miodrag Bulatovic, and Igor Marojevic.

POETRY OF THE PAST

I am a lone straw tossing in
   the whirlwind,
A sad orphan without friend
   or kinfolk.
My people sleep a deep and
   lifeless sleep;
No parent's hand to wipe
   away my tears.
Above my head the heaven is
   shut tight;
It does not hear my cries or
   my prayers. . . .
O my dark day! O my black
   destiny!
O my wretched Serbian
   nation snuffed out!

—from *The Mountain Wreath*
   by Petar Petrovic Njegos

◎ Visual Arts

One of the longest-practiced art forms in Serbia and Montenegro is the painting of icons—sacred images of the saints of the Serbian Orthodox Church. Religious frescoes (paintings done on wet plaster) adorn the walls of churches and monasteries, some estimated to be from the A.D. 900s. Modern artists carry on these traditions, and icons are still displayed in churches, as well as in the homes of most Orthodox Christians.

This is a copy of a detail from **a 1321 fresco.** The original fresco is housed in the Serbian Orthodox Gracanica Monastery's church in Lipljan, Kosovo. In the 1990s, NATO bombs damaged the church, causing the fresco to crack. The copy, unharmed, is in the National Museum of Serbia in Belgrade.

Painters in Serbia and Montenegro also explore a wide range of other subjects. Nadezda Petrovic, who worked in the early 1900s, painted rich, colorful scenes of her homeland and portraits of her neighbors. Katarina Ivanovic also created expressive portraits, while Milic Stankovic used themes from national history and Boza Ilic found inspiration in local landscapes. Petar Lubarda's modern, often abstract, paintings expressed the struggles of the Serbian and Montenegrin people. The turmoil of recent years also influences artists such as Zoran Velimanovic, who says, "I am not gloomy, I am just realistic. I would like [my art] to be different: painting sunset or happy people on a beach eating cakes but in that case I would catch myself lying, and I do not like to lie."

Serbia and Montenegro's artists also work in forms beyond painting. Many photographers used their talent to document the horror of the war. Others used photography to criticize Milosevic and other political leaders. Prominent sculptors include Drinka Radovanovic, who has created many statues of national heroes, from military and political figures to civilian and religious leaders.

Another major area of Serbian and Montenegrin art is known as naive art. This term refers to painting, sculpture, and other works by people who are not trained as artists. This type of art, though usually not as polished as professional art, is popular and important for its freshness and originality. A museum devoted to the genre is located in Jagodina.

***Kolo* dancers** in traditional costumes link arms to begin a demonstration of Serbia and Montenegro's national dance. To learn more about Serbia and Montenegro's culture, go to www.vgsbooks.com for links.

▶ Music and Dance

Serbia and Montenegro has a rich tradition of folk music. Bagpipes called *gajde,* dating back to roughly the fourth century and traditionally made from goatskin, give this music its distinctive sound. Also contributing to that sound is a flute known as the *frula,* or the *zurna* flute popular in Kosovo. Other folk instruments include the violin and accordion. This music is often performed at festivals and other celebrations and is also closely tied to folk dancing, especially the *kolo.* Thought to have Croatian influences, the kolo is known as Serbia and Montenegro's national dance. Kolo dancers stand in a circle and perform steps to the music, often with hands linked or on one another's shoulders.

Just as central to local culture is *blehmuzika,* or "brass music," considered by many people to be the national music. Influenced by the Turkish military trumpets that once sounded across the region, this brassy sound symbolizes Serbia and Montenegro's resistance to invaders. The style varies from place to place. For example, in Kosovo it is influenced more by Turkish and Middle Eastern melodies. In addition, present-day blehmuzika artists such as Boban Markovic adapt their sound to modern musical trends. Some even play at nightclubs and parties. Blehmuzika also takes center stage at a popular summer festival held in Guca, a city south of Belgrade. This annual event has filled Guca's streets with folk dancing, feasting, and partying for more than fifty years.

In addition to these traditional musical styles, rock and other modern genres are also popular in Serbia and Montenegro. Pop stars such as Momcilo Bajagic Bajaga entertain radio audiences and concert crowds. In 2004, when Bajaga's career had spanned twenty years, Serbian crown prince Alexander II honored the anniversary in a letter. The prince praised Bajaga's work, saying that his "songs are a part of all of us, our emotions, history, truth and love."

THE LOCAL BEAT

Many modern music fans in Serbia and Montenegro tune their radios to stations playing Yu-Rock, short for Yugoslavian rock and roll. This musical style had origins in the 1950s but gained power and popularity during the 1980s, when many artists used the genre to speak out against Milosevic. With a growingly tense political situation and the NATO bombings of the 1990s, Yu-Rock came to symbolize the people's unity and their protest against both the repressive government and the bombings.

Serbia and Montenegro's royal family—which in modern times serves a primarily symbolic role—is descended from both the famous revolutionary Karageorge and from the Montenegrin royal house of Petrovic-Njegos. They are also related to royal families in Russia, Great Britain, and Denmark.

◉ Food

Serbian and Montenegrin cuisine has been influenced by the same combination of invasion, location, and tradition as the rest of its culture—resulting in delicious local fare. The hearty starches and meat dishes of Eastern Europe are common.

Diners enjoy a meal in the open air at a café in central Belgrade.

Nearby Mediterranean nations add flavors of garlic, feta cheese, and even the occasional hot pepper.

The nation suffered from severe food shortages in the aftermath of recent wars. International aid organizations such as the United Nations World Food Program provided emergency food supplies for as many as 700,000 hungry people. With the help of these outside agencies, the crisis had lessened significantly by 2004.

When food is readily available, meat dishes are common on Serbian and Montenegrin tables. Favorites include smoked ham, sausages, and *pljeskavica* (Serbian "hamburger," usually made of ground beef and sometimes lamb, seasoned with onions and hot pepper or paprika, and served plain or on pita bread). Meat also appears in entrées including stuffed peppers, shish kebabs, *sarma* (cabbage leaves stuffed with rice and ground meat), and Hungarian goulash (a thick stew flavored with paprika). Fish is featured in recipes such as *alaska corba*, a hearty stew often prepared in homes along the Danube.

The cheese pie known as *gibanica* is another traditional meal. It is made of thin layers of buttery dough soaked with an egg mixture and baked to a golden brown. *Burek* is a similar favorite, layering dough with fillings such as meat, fruit, or cheese.

GIBANICA (CHEESE PIE)

This Serbian classic is popular throughout the federation. Local cooks often make the dough from scratch, and some also use a special kind of cheese that is hard to find outside of the Balkan Peninsula. However, this simpler version is still delicious.

1 lb. feta cheese, chopped very finely

2 c. small curd cottage cheese

6 eggs, beaten

1 c. milk

½ lb. prepared phyllo dough

2 tbsp. butter, sliced into thin pats

1. Preheat oven to 400°F.
2. Mix feta, cottage cheese, eggs, and milk in a large bowl. Stir well.
3. Cover the bottom of a greased rectangular baking dish with two or three layers of phyllo dough. (You will probably need to use several "leaves," or pieces, of phyllo for each layer.)
4. Dip a leaf of phyllo into the cheese mixture, coating it well. Lay the leaf in the dish, wrinkling it a little so that it doesn't lie quite flat. Repeat, spreading leaves evenly over the bottom of the dish, until you have only enough phyllo left to cover the top.
5. Place remaining phyllo leaves over the top. Place butter pats on top of this layer, and spoon any extra cheese mixture over all. Bake 35 to 40 minutes, or until the top is golden and a knife inserted near the center of the pie comes out clean. Cut into diamonds or squares and serve.

Serves 8 to 10

Appetizers and side dishes are often vegetarian, such as the standard Serbian salad of tomatoes, onions, green peppers, and cucumbers. Other favorites are grilled peppers, fresh cabbage salad, tangy yogurt and cucumber sauce, and fried cheese. Bread is a part of every Serbian and Montenegrin meal and may be made from wheat, barley, or millet. Local bakers also make a corn bread known as *proja*. The flat pocket bread *pogaca* is often prepared for special occasions and sometimes filled with sour cream for an extra treat. For dessert, a variety of cakes, cookies, chocolates, and fresh fruit are popular. Another favorite is *palacinke*—thin, sweet pancakes rolled up around fruit, sweet cheese, chocolate sauce, or chopped nuts. Palacinke can be a breakfast food as well.

▶ Sports and Recreation

Sporting events are a great pastime in Serbia and Montenegro. Soccer—called football by the locals—is one of the most beloved sports. Thousands of fans turn out to watch Belgrade's two teams, Red Star and Partizan. Montenegro, in particular, is known for producing outstanding players, such as Ivica Kralj, Dejan Savicevic, and Predrag Mijatovic.

Partizan Belgrade soccer player Simon Vukcevic (right) struggles to keep the ball away from a player on Romania's Dinamo Bucarest team.

A **basketball player** (right) for Serbia and Montenegro has control of the ball in a game against Italy at the 2004 Summer Olympics in Athens, Greece.

Basketball is another favorite sport. An American visitor introduced the game to Serbia and Montenegro in the 1920s, and it quickly caught on. Even though many star players have left home to play professionally in the United States, teams from Serbia and Montenegro consistently do well in European competitions and beyond.

Athletes from Serbia and Montenegro have competed in the Olympic Games, on both Yugoslavian and Serbian and Montenegrin teams. Not surprisingly, soccer and basketball have been strong sports for the country, and the men's volleyball team—nicknamed the Balkan Blues for the color of their uniforms—has also done well. In the 2004 Summer Games in Athens, Greece, Serbia and Montenegro won two silver medals, one in men's water polo and the other in a women's shooting event.

Other forms of fun and relaxation in Serbia and Montenegro include movies, live theater, and parties or nightclubs. When staying in, many people enjoy watching television. Although Milosevic's administration strictly controlled programming, restraints have loosened dramatically. Many shows from the United States and other countries have gained broad audiences in Serbia and Montenegro.

THE ECONOMY

Like all nations that have been through war or other turmoil, Serbia and Montenegro has struggled to get its economy back on track. More than a decade of on-and-off conflict brought crippling economic sanctions, massive military spending, and the devastation of precious resources. Industrial and agricultural production plummeted. And especially during Milosevic's reign, widespread corruption and mismanagement also slowed economic growth. Organized crime thrived during the worst years of the sanctions, when goods that could no longer be imported legally showed up on the black market at hugely inflated prices. In fact, inflation as a whole skyrocketed, dealing yet another damaging blow to the economy.

Meanwhile, the Communist government explored privatization—shifting the ownership of companies and other assets to individuals rather than the government. The government hoped the change would boost the lagging economy. However, the process has encountered many obstacles, including resistance from workers who fear the loss of

their jobs, and unfair treatment by government officials and others who prefer to keep assets centrally concentrated. As a result, less than half of Serbia and Montenegro's businesses have been privatized. The changeover has yet to improve Serbia and Montenegro's financial situation dramatically.

Nevertheless, the loosening of international sanctions, as well as several years of peace, has brightened Serbia and Montenegro's economic outlook. But old problems linger, such as inflation, which—while far below the 3,000-percent high that it hit at one point—still frequently reaches double digits. Meanwhile, the nation suffers high unemployment rates, which have hovered around 25 to 35 percent ever since the late 1990s. While high, these figures are much lower than the mid-1990s high of 60 percent. For all of these reasons, Serbia and Montenegro has relied heavily on international aid since Milosevic's exit from office. Government leaders have also made efforts to boost the economy with measures including joining the

International Monetary Fund, the European Bank for Reconstruction and Development, and other international economic organizations.

At times, the separate republics of Serbia and Montenegro have clashed over political issues, which have occasionally spilled over into economic concerns. For example, each republic periodically placed trade restrictions on the other when still part of Yugoslavia. Although Serbia has generally been the more powerful of the republics, Montenegro has made a strong stand for both political and economic independence. As part of this effort, Montenegro has kept its currency separate from Serbia's, adopting the European euro, while the official national currency of the federation as a whole is the dinar.

Additionally, Kosovo—under continuing international supervision but still an autonomous part of the federation—has a semi-independent economic system. Outside aid has flowed into this troubled region, but it remains the least developed of Serbia and Montenegro's provinces. It continues to be a drain on the federation's financial resources.

◉ Trade and Services

Because of economic sanctions and the need for reconstruction in the wake of the war, Serbia and Montenegro has had to import more goods than it exports. This mounting trade deficit had grown to more than $7 billion by 2004.

However, the nation's exports have risen steadily since the turn of the century. National economic leaders are striving to reduce this gap even further. Among Serbia and Montenegro's main exports are fresh fruits and vegetables, chemical products, and manufactured goods. One of its main imports is fuel. Other imported goods include machinery and food products. Major trading partners include Germany, Bosnia-Herzegovina, Italy, Hungary, and Greece.

Domestically, Serbia and Montenegro's service sector supports 35 to 40 percent of the nation's workforce. This wide-ranging area of the economy includes workers from sales-people to teachers and health-care employees. It makes up about 57 percent of Serbia and Montenegro's GDP. Private shopkeepers, restaurant owners and workers, and hotel employees also fall into the service sector.

One aspect of the services is tourism, which—given the federation's volatile recent history—was lagging badly in the early 2000s. As peace takes a firmer hold, however, businesspeople in the region hope that Serbia and Montenegro's natural beauty and historical sites will attract travelers once again.

The communications industry—one aspect of the service sector—is expanding its reach in Serbia and Montenegro. In the early 2000s, the number of phones per 100 people was estimated at 49—higher than neighboring nations but still low compared to many European countries. Similarly, with about 6 percent of residents using the Internet, Serbia and Montenegro is improving its communications systems, but it still has far to go to catch up to most developed nations.

White-water rapids on the Tara River in Montenegro challenge a pair of tourists. Many historical sights also can attract tourists to Serbia and Montenegro.

Industry and Mining

Industry makes up more than one-quarter of Serbia and Montenegro's gross domestic product (GDP)—the total annual value of goods and services produced within the country's borders. It employs about 40 percent of the federation's workforce. In the early 2000s, the sector also began to show slow growth rates.

Factories in Belgrade, Novi Pazar, Beocin, and other industrial centers produce manufactured goods ranging from cars and tractors to machinery and building materials. Metallurgy—the production and processing of metals including iron, steel, and aluminum—makes up a significant portion of the federation's industry. Other areas of manufacture include chemicals, electronics, food products, and textiles.

Mining is also important to Serbia and Montenegro's economy. Copper is one of the most significant resources. The nation is home to some of Europe's largest reserves of copper ore and boasts an ancient history of mining the metal. Coal is another valuable natural resource, as are iron, lead, nickel, silver, and gold.

ANCIENT INDUSTRY

Mining—a mainstay of modern Serbia and Montenegro's economy—has a regional history thousands of years old. Rudna Glava, a mine southeast of Belgrade, was unearthed in 1968 and is believed to have begun operating approximately six to seven thousand years ago. Nearby, at the town of Majdanpek, is one of the oldest mines still in operation. Opened at least six centuries ago, Majdanpek—yielding gold and copper—remained active on and off under Ottoman rule and beyond. Most present-day residents of Majdanpek are still miners, and the town is home to a mining museum exploring this local industry.

This coal mine is near Lazarevac in central Serbia. Mining continues to be important to Serbia and Montenegro's economy in modern times.

Serbia and Montenegro is the third-largest producer of **plums** in the world. Each year about 44,000 plum trees yield 400,000 tons (363,000 metric tons) of plums.

◉ Agriculture, Forestry, and Fishing

Once the cornerstone of the regional economy, agriculture has been largely surpassed by industrial activities in profitability. It makes up only about 15 percent of the GDP. However, farming still employs approximately 20 to 25 percent of Serbia and Montenegro's laborers, most of whom live and work on small, family-owned farms. The sector has also shown promising growth, with production increasing nearly 20 percent from 2003 to 2004.

> Vojvodina's flat, open plains allow the use of mechanized farming equipment such as tractors. However, many of these vehicles are old and in poor condition. In the Republic of Serbia, the average tractor is more than ten years old.

Roughly 35 percent of Serbia and Montenegro's total land is arable, or suitable for farming. Most of this land is in Serbia proper, with the most heavily farmed region being Vojvodina, on the rich, fertile soil of the plains stretching away from the Danube. These wide plains are perfect for raising grain crops such as corn and wheat. Sugar beets, potatoes, and other vegetables also grow well there.

Beyond the plains, in the nation's hillier areas, fruit is a major crop. Local farmers tend orchards of apricots, peaches, and pears, and the region is famed for its juicy plums. Vineyards, especially in Montenegro, provide harvests of grapes, and the region is known for its wines.

Sales of **poultry** products in Serbia and Montenegro, such as those from this farm near Valjevo, dropped by up to 50 percent in March 2006. That month a deadly strain of bird flu was found in a rooster in Bajina Basta in western Serbia.

Many farmers also keep livestock, including cattle, pigs, and chickens. Sheep and goats are well suited to Montenegro, where much of the mountainous terrain is too rough for cattle herds.

Although Serbia and Montenegro was once thickly forested, forestry makes up a relatively small part of the modern federation's overall economy and is concentrated primarily in Montenegro. However, in 2003 the country launched the National Forest Programme of Serbia with the help of the Forestry and Agriculture Organization (FAO). This project aims to revitalize Serbia and Montenegro's forestry sector.

Fishing also contributes to the economy, but catches are relatively small. They consist largely of freshwater fish caught in the Danube and other rivers. Montenegro's coastline provides catches of saltwater seafood including bluefish. In addition, aquaculture—the raising of fish in farms—yields about 4,400 tons (3,992 metric tons) of carp annually.

For the latest information about the economy of Serbia and Montenegro, go to www.vgsbooks.com for links.

Transportation and Energy

Nearly all forms of transportation in Serbia and Montenegro were damaged in wartime, especially during the NATO bombings of 1999. For example, some stretches of the nation's railroads are still being rebuilt. Nevertheless, the Belgrade-Bar Railway and other legs of the federation's rail system—totaling more than 2,400 miles (3,862 km) of track—remain vital to the movement of both goods and passengers. In addition, more than 30,000 miles (48,279 km) of highways—approximately one-third of that distance unpaved—crisscross the country.

Montenegro, with its short but valuable coastline, is the hub of the federation's sea traffic. Bar, Kotor, and Herceg Novi are important coastal ports. Bar's facilities alone are capable of handling about 5 million tons (4.5 million metric tons) of cargo annually. River traffic is busy at Belgrade, Novi Sad, and other cities along the Danube and Sava. International airports in Belgrade and Podgorica also serve travelers and shippers.

The Belgrade-Bar Railway line connects Belgrade with Bar on the Adriatic coast—a distance of 292 miles (467 km). Here the tracks pass near Valjevo in western Serbia.

One area of ongoing concern is energy supply. Maintenance problems have slowed electrical output, and—even as demand rises—production has dropped. The result is an overall energy deficit, with Serbia and Montenegro's power plants meeting only about one-fourth of the population's needs. Outages are common, and the nation is forced to import most of its fuel. This situation is most critical during the winter, when households, especially in the north, need more power for heat.

While Serbia and Montenegro does have reserves of oil and coal, these resources are not expected to last much beyond mid-century. Hydroelectric power has been slow to develop. Because of these challenges, the use of natural gas—through both Serbia and Montenegro's reserves and the building of new pipelines to import the fuel—is likely to grow.

Power lines carry electricity in Novi Sad when it is available. Outages are common all over Serbia and Montenegro.

Catch up on the latest news in Serbia and Montenegro, including new developments as Montenegro gains independence and Kosovo considers taking the same path. For links go to www.vgsbooks.com.

The Future

With a long and vibrant past but a painful recent history of war and bitter conflict, Serbia and Montenegro's story is one of drama and difficulty. And its story is far from over. The federation seems on the brink of dissolving, following Montenegro's May 2006 vote to become independent and with Kosovo working to take similar steps. Up to one-third of the land's people are still estimated to live in poverty, and the burden of international debt weighs heavily. International investment in Serbian and Montenegrin business—seen by many economic experts as vital to the federation's financial success—has been slow, due in part to the region's uncertain conditions. Meanwhile, the dinar is still struggling to remain stable, and inflation continues to drag the economy down.

But many changes offer second chances for Serbia and Montenegro. Economically, privatization efforts slowly continue and have advanced especially successfully in Montenegro. The GDP is beginning to grow again, and exports are up. Politically, fresh leadership, peace among diverse ethnic and religious groups, and economic security offer new opportunities for stability and harmony. And with its valued tradition of national pride and fierce individuality, Serbia and Montenegro has the potential to write a much brighter future for itself and for all of its people.

CA. 6000 B.C.   The Starcevo culture emerges around the Danube
                 River.

CA. 3800 B.C.   Vinca civilization reaches its peak.

200s B.C.   The Celts create a settlement near the future site of Belgrade.

A.D. 100s   Armies of the Roman Empire settle the Balkan Peninsula.

395   The Roman Empire splits and the future Serbia and Montenegro
                 becomes part of the Byzantine Empire.

400s–500s   Invaders attack the Byzantine Empire.

600s   The Serbs settle the region that will become Serbia and Montenegro.

800s   Vlastimir accepts Byzantine rule in order to fight off Bulgar invaders.

1054   The Christian church splits into Roman Catholic and the Eastern Orthodox
                 branches.

1169   Prince Stefan Nemanja takes power.

1217   King Stefan Prvovencani is crowned.

1349   Dusan's Code of laws is introduced.

1389   Balkan forces are defeated by the Ottomans at Kosovo Polje. Prince Lazar is
                 killed in battle.

1500s–1600s   The system of devshirme forces thousands of Christian Serbian sons to con-
                 vert to Islam.

1754   Bishop Vasilije Petrovic publishes a history of Montenegro.

1804   George Petrovic (Karageorge) leads a revolt against Ottoman rule.

1812   The Treaty of Bucharest gives Serbia limited freedom.

1830s   Prince Milos Obrenovic introduces widespread reforms, but his strict rule
                 provokes rebellion.

1847   Petar Petrovic Njegos publishes his masterpiece, *The Mountain Wreath*.

1869   A new constitution is adopted.

1875   Ottoman and Balkan Peninsula forces go to war.

1882   King Milan Obrenovic II declares Serbia a kingdom.

1912   The first Balkan War breaks out.

1914   Archduke Franz Ferdinand of Austria-Hungary is assassi-
                 nated in Sarajevo. World War I erupts.

1915 Serbia is captured by the armies of the Central powers. Thousands of refugees die in an attempt to escape.

1916 The Central powers take Montenegro.

1918 The Kingdom of Serbs, Croats, and Slovenes is officially formed.

1929 King Alexander declares absolute rule and renames the nation Yugoslavia.

1939 World War II begins.

1941 Yugoslavia is occupied by the Axis powers. Internal attacks, ethnic cleansing, and civil war tear the nation apart.

1945 World War II ends. Josip Broz (Tito) becomes the leader of Yugoslavia.

1968 Antigovernment protests erupt in Belgrade. Riots break out in Kosovo and Macedonia.

1974 Tito introduces a new constitution, designed to hold Yugoslavia together after his death.

1980 Tito dies.

1984 Sarajevo hosts the Winter Olympics.

1989 Slobodan Milosevic is elected president of the Serbian Republic.

1992 Following the independence of Slovenia, Macedonia, Croatia, and Bosnia-Herzegovina, the new Federal Republic of Yugoslavia is formed.

1994 NATO bombs Serbia in retaliation for Serbian actions in Bosnia.

1997–1998 War erupts in Kosovo. Milosevic sends troops into the region.

1999 NATO bombs Serbia once more.

2000 Milosevic is defeated by Vojislav Kostunica in national elections.

2002 The federation of Serbia and Montenegro is created. Milosevic goes on trial before a UN war crimes tribunal (court).

2004 Renewed fighting breaks out in Kosovo.

2005 Montenegrin president Filip Vujanovic proposes considering independence for the federation's republics before the 2006 deadline.

2006 As Milosevic's war crimes trial nears its conclusion in March, he dies of a heart attack. In May, Montenegro holds a referendum in which voters choose to separate from Serbia. The vote begins the process by which Montenegro will become independent.

COUNTRY NAME Serbia and Montenegro

AREA 39,448 square miles (102,170 sq. km)

MAIN LANDFORMS Pannonian Plain, Balkan Mountains, Dinaric Alps, Kopaonik massif, Southwestern Coastal Plains, Northern Plains, karst region

HIGHEST POINT Mount Daravica, 8,714 feet (2,656 m) above sea level

MAJOR RIVERS Danube, Sava, Tisza, Morava, Drina

ANIMALS Bears, chamois, deer, Dinaric voles, lynxes, pine martens, wild boars, wolves

CAPITAL CITY Belgrade

OTHER MAJOR CITIES Novi Sad, Pristina, Podgorica, Nis, Novi Pazar, Subotica, Niksic, Herceg Novi, Kotor, Cetinje, Bar

OFFICIAL LANGUAGE Serbian

MONETARY UNIT dinar. 1 dinar = 100 paras. (In Montenegro and Kosovo, the euro is used in place of the dinar. 1 euro = 100 cents.)

SERBIAN AND MONTENEGRIN CURRENCIES

The official currency of Serbia is the dinar. Made up of 100 paras, this currency dates back to the early 1200s and the rule of Stefan Prvovencani. Later, the dinar also served as the national currency of the Kingdom of Serbs, Croats, and Slovenes, and of Yugoslavia.

Although Montenegro shared the dinar during most of its years as part of Yugoslavia, the modern republic has adopted the euro in its place. The euro is an international currency used by most nations in the European Union (EU). Although Montenegro is not part of the EU, it is permitted to use the euro. The euro is also used in Kosovo.

In the Republic of Serbia, bills are printed in denominations of 10, 20, 50, 100 *(above)*, 200, 500, 1,000, and 5,000 dinars, and coins are minted in values of 50 paras and 1, 2, 5, 10, and 20 dinars. Euros are issued in bills valued at 5, 10, 20, 50, 100, 200, and 500 euros, and in coins of 1, 2, 5, 10, 20, and 50 cents, and 1 and 2 euros.

The official flag of the federation of Serbia and Montenegro is composed of three horizontal bands of equal height. From the top to the bottom, they are blue, white, and red. In addition to this shared flag, the individual republics of Serbia and Montenegro have their own flags. Serbia's state flag is similar to the federation flag, with the same colors in three bands. However, on the Serbian flag, the red band is on the top, blue is in the middle, and white is on the bottom. Serbia's state flag also has a coat of arms just to the left of the flag's center, showing a two-headed eagle, a crown, and a royal crest. Montenegro's flag has a gold border and a red background. In the center rests a coat of arms somewhat similar to Serbia's. The Montenegrin coat of arms also features the two-headed eagle and a crown, but this eagle holds a scepter and an orb (sphere) in its talons, and the crest in the center is different from Serbia's.

The federation has one joint national anthem, while each republic has one of its own. The federal anthem is "Hej Sloveni" or "Hey Slavs." Formerly the anthem of Yugoslavia, the song has lyrics written by Samuel Tomasik in the mid-1800s. The lyrics are set to a melody by an unknown composer. The first verse of the anthem appears below.

Hey Slavs—
The spirit of your grandfathers still lives,
While for their people beat the hearts
Of their sons.

In August 2004, the Republic of Serbia chose "Boze Pravde" (God of Justice), with music composed by Davorin Jenko and words by Jovan Djordjevic, as its state anthem. Similarly, Montenegro adopted "Oj svijetla majska zoro" (Oh Bright Dawn of May) in July 2004.

To listen to Serbia and Montenegro's national anthem, go to www.vgsbooks.com for links.

JOSIP BROZ, AKA TITO (1892–1980) Broz was born in Kumrovec, a town that was, over the years, part of Austria-Hungary, the Kingdom of Serbs, Croats, and Slovenes, Yugoslavia, and modern Croatia. Broz—known as Tito—would go on to become a critical figure in Serbian history. After working various jobs as a young man, he became deeply involved in politics. As an organizer of Partisan resistance forces during World War II, Tito became the leader of postwar Yugoslavia. Introducing a modified version of Communism to the nation, Tito governed with tactics that were often controversial. Nevertheless, he was one of the country's most important leaders.

LAZAR HREBELJANOVIC (ca. 1329–1389) Born in Prilepac, Kosovo, Lazar was the son of an officer of King Dusan's court. Lazar, too, went on to hold posts in government, and he advanced quickly. By the 1360s, he had been named a prince, and beginning in about 1371, he was Serbia's primary leader. But the prince's life came to an abrupt end at the Battle of Kosovo Polje in 1389, when Ottoman soldiers killed and beheaded him. Lazar left the Kneginja (Princess) Milica as his widow. Few details of Milica's life are known, but she ruled briefly after his death and was praised for the famously moving poem of mourning that she wrote for her husband. Lazar soon became a Serbian legend, representing his people's brave struggles against conquerors.

MILEVA MARIC (1875–1948) Maric was born in Titel, Vojvodina, to a wealthy family. She displayed a remarkable talent for mathematics and science at a young age. In 1896 she became one of the first female students to attend the Swiss Federal Polytechnic, a school in Zurich, Switzerland. There she met and fell in love with a fellow student named Albert Einstein. The couple married in 1903, and Maric soon had to devote her time to caring for their children. Meanwhile, Einstein developed and published the scientific theories that made him famous. To this day, historians disagree over whether Maric helped him in this work and, if so, how much she contributed. Einstein and Maric—who divorced in 1919—never said, and the mystery still intrigues many.

NATASA MICIC (b. 1965) Born in Uzice, a city in western Serbia and Montenegro, Micic began her career as a lawyer. She soon became involved in her nation's politics, rising quickly to a post as president of Serbia's national assembly. Then, in December 2002, Micic took over as the republic's acting president after two elections failed to fill the office. She thus became both the first woman to hold the Serbian presidency and—at the age of thirty-seven—the youngest person to do so. In February 2003, after the assassination of Prime Minister Djindic, Micic declared a state of emergency. The move was controversial but prevented widespread violence. She occupied the presidential post until early 2004, when new elections brought Boris Tadic to office. However, she remains active in Serbia and Montenegro's government.

STEFAN NEMANJA (ca. 1113–1200) Born in Podgorica, Nemanja became grand zupan of Serbia in about 1168. He went on to win great military successes, expanding Serbia's territory with the capture of lands including much of Kosovo. He also contributed much to learning and religion in his realm by sponsoring the building of many churches and monasteries, including the famous Studenica Monastery near Novi Pazar. In about 1196, he turned the throne of the Nemanjic dynasty over to his middle son (also named Stefan) and became a monk. Nemanja's youngest son, Rastko, was also a monk. Rastko, who became known as Saint Sava, is remembered as the founder of the independent Serbian church and its first archbishop (a high-ranking religious official).

MILORAD PAVIC (b. 1929) Pavic, born in Belgrade, is one of Serbia and Montenegro's most widely acclaimed writers. His dense, complex works explore many elements of Serbian and Montenegrin history and culture. He has written short stories, poetry, and essays, and his novels include *Dictionary of the Khazars, A Landscape Painted with Tea,* and *Last Love in Constantinople*. His works have been translated into many languages, and he has translated the works of European poets into Serbo-Croatian. In addition, he is a scholar of historical Serbian literature. Pavic's wife, Jasmina Mihajlovic, is also an author.

DUSKO POPOV (1912–1981) Popov, born into a wealthy Serb family, led a life of such adventure that he is believed to have been the real-life inspiration for the book and movie character James Bond. In 1940, as World War II enveloped Europe, Germany's military intelligence agency recruited Popov as a spy. Although he was actually deeply opposed to the Nazi government, he accepted the job. He then quickly offered the British his services as a double agent. Popov proved to be an excellent spy. He spoke five languages, was known for his charm, and concocted espionage tools such as invisible ink. Although he frequently got in trouble with authorities for his outrageous private life, he was one of the war's most important secret agents and contributed significantly to the Allies' eventual victory.

DEJAN SAVICEVIC (b. 1966) Born in Podgorica, Savicevic began playing soccer in national youth leagues at the age of fifteen. He soon became one of Serbia and Montenegro's most popular and praised soccer stars, playing midfield first for the Titograd (Podgorica) team and then for Belgrade. Beginning in 1992, he spent five seasons with AC Milan, one of Italy's famous soccer teams. He also took part in two World Cup tournaments for Yugoslavia. After retiring in the late 1990s, Savicevic went on to coach Yugoslavia's and later Serbia and Montenegro's team, taking a squad to the 2002 World Cup.

Sights to See

Serbia and Montenegro's complex history and lovely landscape have given the country many sights to visit. But instability still makes Serbia and Montenegro a dangerous destination for tourists. Anyone considering traveling to Serbia and Montenegro should first check with the U.S. State Department (see the website at http://travel.state .gov/travel_warnings.html) and with embassies in Serbia and Montenegro to determine the safety of visiting the region.

BELGRADE Serbia and Montenegro's capital city offers a wealth of options for any visitor. For history buffs and art lovers, the National Museum is a must-see, while the Bajrakli Mosque and the Orthodox Cathedral offer additional insights into Serbia and Montenegro's history and culture. Animal lovers should stop by the Belgrade Zoo, conveniently located in the Kalemegdan—an Ottoman fortress turned into a public park that is perfect for a stroll. For shopping and dining, Knez Mihajlova and Skadarlia streets are the hottest spots in town.

FORTRESSES OF THE DANUBE Throughout the centuries, many fortresses have been built in Serbia and Montenegro to protect precious territory along the Danube River. One of the most notable examples is Golubac Fortress, perched near the Iron Gate—a rocky gorge along the Serbian-Romanian border. Golubac, believed to have been built by Hungarian forces, boasts more than six hundred years of history. Smederevo Fortress, outside of Belgrade, is famous for being the last hold-out against Ottoman invaders in the 1400s, while the foundations of Novi Sad's massive Petrovaradin Citadel date back to the Roman era.

KOTOR This coastal Montenegrin city is one of the best-preserved medieval towns in the Balkans. The United Nations Educational, Scientific, and Cultural Organization lists the city as a World Heritage site. Kotor's historical treasures include ninth-century city gates, twelfth-century churches, and fourteenth-century palaces. The city also offers stunning views of both the sea and the mountains.

LEPENSKI VIR Located in eastern Serbia's Djerdap National Park, archaeologists unearthed this ancient site in the 1960s. Comprising the remains of a settlement believed to be seven to eight thousand years old, Lepenski Vir is one of the most important archaeological sites in Europe.

ORTHODOX MONUMENTS Serbia and Montenegro, with a strong tradition of Orthodoxy, is dotted with hundreds of churches, monasteries, and convents. The Gracanica Monastery near Pristina, Ravanica (one of many churches founded by Prince Lazar) stands outside of Belgrade, while the Studenica Monastery (founded by Stefan Nemanja) is near Novi Pazar. Other highlights include the Patriarchate of Pec (a complex of four churches in western Kosovo), Savina Monastery near Herceg Novi, and Ostrog Monastery, set into a cliff northwest of Podgorica.

Communism: a political and economic model based on the idea of common, rather than private, property. In a Communist system, the government controls most goods and services.

genocide: the planned and systematic killing of a group of people based on their race, religion, or other cultural features. Genocide is also called ethnic cleansing. The Holocaust of World War II was an example of genocide. Genocide also took place in Serbia and Montenegro and other Balkan nations during the wars of the 1990s.

inflation: an increase in the price of goods relative to the value of the national currency

internally displaced people (IDP): citizens who have fled from their homes because of danger or persecution but who remain within the border of their home country

Islam: a religion founded on the Arabian Peninsula in the seventh century A.D. by the prophet Muhammad. The religion's primary tenets are known as the Five Pillars of Islam. Most followers of Islam, called Muslims, are members of the Sunni sect, while others follow the Shiite branch of the religion.

nationalism: a philosophy that values loyalty to one's own nation above all else. Nationalist goals may include preservation of national culture, fulfillment of the nation's needs, and the nation's independence from outside influence.

Orthodox Christianity: also called Eastern Orthodoxy, this religion is a branch of Christianity that broke off from the Roman Catholic Church in 1054. Many residents of Serbia and Montenegro follow Eastern Orthodox Christianity.

peasant: a farmer and, usually, member of a low-ranking social class

privatization: the transfer of ownership of businesses, goods, and other assets from government (public) to individual (private) control

refugee: a person who has been forced to flee his or her home country to escape danger

Slavs: members of an ethnic group, sometimes called a tribe, that was believed to originate in eastern Europe. Slavs share a language family as well as an historical background.

Titoism: the kind of Communism employed by Josip Broz (Tito), Yugoslavia's leader from 1945 to 1980. Titoism did not follow the style and pattern of Soviet Communism and was generally less restrictive.

United Nations: an international organization formed at the end of World War II in 1945 to help handle global disputes. The United Nations replaced a similar, earlier group known as the League of Nations.

Glossary

Selected Bibliography

Cable News Network. *CNN.com*. 2005. http://www.cnn.com (February 16, 2005).
This site provides current events and breaking news about Serbia and Montenegro, as well as a searchable archive of older articles.

CIA. *The World Factbook: Serbia and Montenegro*. 2004. http://www.cia.gov/cia/publications/factbook/geos/yi.html (February 16, 2005).
This source offers statistics and background information on Serbia and Montenegro's economy, history, demographics, and more.

Clissold, Stephen, ed. *A Short History of Yugoslavia: From Early Times to 1966*. Cambridge, UK: Cambridge University Press, 1966.
This survey offers useful information on Serbia and Montenegro's history as Yugoslavia, ending about midway through Tito's time in power.

Cox, John K. *The History of Serbia*. Westport, CT: Greenwood Press, 2002.
This book provides a moderately detailed overview of Serbian and Montenegrin history.

Dyker, David A. "Yugoslavia: Economy." In *Regional Surveys of the World: Central and South-Eastern Europe*, 580–582. London: Europa Publications, 2003.
This article examines the recent economic situation in the former Yugoslavia, including Serbia and Montenegro.

Europa World Yearbook, 2003. Vol. 2. London: Europa Publications, 2003.
Covering Serbia and Montenegro's recent history, economy, and government, this annual publication also provides a wealth of statistics on population, employment, trade, and more.

Judah, Tim. *The Serbs: History, Myth, and the Destruction of Yugoslavia*. New Haven, CT: Yale University Press, 1997.
This book explores Serbian identity and its relationship to the wars of the twentieth century.

Mijatovic, Chedomil. *Servia of the Servians*. New York: Charles Scribner's Sons, 1915.
This book examines the history and especially the culture of Serbia.

NIP (Novinsko Izdavacko Preduzece, or Press Publishing Company). *Illustrated History of the Serbs*. 1999. http://www.snaga.org.yu/Ilustrovana_istorija_srba/tekst/engleski/01/01-uvod.html (February 25, 2005).
This online publication surveys Serbian history from prehistoric times up to the fateful 1389 battle of Kosovo Polje.

Norris, David. "Yugoslavia: History." *Regional Surveys of the World: Central and South-Eastern Europe*, 572–579. London: Europa Publications, 2003.
This article surveys the recent history of the former Yugoslavia, including Serbia and Montenegro.

Population Reference Bureau. "2004 World Population Data Sheet." *Population Reference Bureau (PRB).* **2004.**
http://www.prb.org/pdf04/04WorldDataSheet_Eng.pdf (February 16, 2005).
This annual statistics sheet provides a wealth of data on Serbia and Montenegro's population, birth and death rates, fertility rate, infant mortality rate, and other useful demographic information.

Project Rastko. "The History of Serbian Culture." *Internet Library of Serb Culture.* **2004.**
http://www.rastko.org.yu/isk/index_e.html (February 25, 2004).
This site offers the text of a book on Serbian culture, with details on art, music, literature, and more.

ReliefWeb. "Countries and Emergencies: Serbia and Montenegro." *ReliefWeb.* **2004.**
http://www.reliefweb.int/rw/dbc.nsf/doc104?OpenForm&rc=4&cc=scm (February 21, 2005).
This site presents information on humanitarian concerns in Serbia and Montenegro, including food supply, land mines, and more.

Serbian Unity Congress. **2004.**
http://www.suc.org/ (February 21, 2005).
This website provides a wealth of articles and information on Serbian history and culture, from major political figures of the past to current events.

Turner, Barry, ed. *The Statesman's Yearbook: The Politics, Cultures, and Economies of the World, 2003.* **New York: Macmillan Press, 2003.**
This resource provides concise information on Serbia and Montenegro's history, climate, government, economy, and culture, including relevant statistics.

U.S. Department of State: Bureau of European and Eurasian Affairs. "Serbia and Montenegro." *Background Notes.* **2004.**
http://www.state.gov/r/pa/ei/bgn/5388.htm (February 22, 2005).
This overview, published annually and regularly updated by the U.S. government, provides an introduction to Serbia and Montenegro's government, history, foreign relations, and more.

The World Bank Group. *Serbia and Montenegro Country Brief.* **2002.**
http://lnweb18.worldbank.org/eca/eca.nsf/Countries/Yugoslavia/
A2AA7CE96EC98FF285256C24005408BD?OpenDocumen (February 16, 2005).
This World Bank website surveys Serbia and Montenegro's economy.

Further Reading and Websites

Andryszewski, Tricia. *Kosovo: The Splintering of Yugoslavia.* Brookfield, CT: Millbrook Press, 2000.
This book describes the war in Kosovo and its aftermath, especially the experiences of refugees.

Benson, Michael. *Bill Clinton.* Minneapolis: Lerner Publications Company, 2004.
This biography of former president Bill Clinton includes information on Clinton's controversial decision to support and encourage the 1999 NATO air strikes on Yugoslavia.

Blue, Rose, and Corinne J. Naden. *Monica Seles.* Philadelphia: Chelsea House Publishers, 2002.
This biography tells the story of Monica Seles, who was born in Novi Sad and went on to become a world-class tennis champion.

Country Profile: Serbia and Montenegro.
http://news.bbc.co.uk/1/hi/world/europe/country_profiles/1039269.stm
The BBC online presents an overview of Serbia and Montenegro, complete with a timeline, map, and links to breaking news.

Englar, Mary. *Bosnia-Herzegovina in Pictures.* Minneapolis: Twenty-First Century Books, 2007.
This book provides an overview of the history, culture, and geography of Bosnia-Herzegovina, Serbia and Montenegro's neighbor and part of the former Yugoslavia.

Goldstein, Margaret J. *World War II: Europe.* Minneapolis: Lerner Publications Company, 2004.
This book presents a history of World War II's European battles, with a focus on U.S. involvement.

Marcovitz, Hal. *The Balkans: People in Conflict.* Philadelphia: Chelsea House, 2002.
This book examines the troubled recent history of the Balkan Peninsula.

The New York Times on the Web.
http://www.nytimes.com
This online version of the newspaper offers current news stories along with an archive of articles on Serbia and Montenegro.

Podgorica.
http://www.podgorica.cg.yu
This website presents information on the history, culture, and other facets of Montenegro's capital city.

Ruggiero, Adriane. *The Ottoman Empire.* New York: Benchmark Books, 2003.
Explore the powerful Ottoman Empire, which controlled and influenced Serbia and Montenegro for more than five hundred years.

Schiffman, Ruth. *Josip Broz Tito.* New York: Chelsea House, 1987.
This biography explores the life and political career of Tito.

Serbia Info: Explore Serbia.
http://www.serbia-info.com/enc/explore.html
Check out this site for information on sights to see and cultural attractions in the Republic of Serbia.

Serbia and Montenegro.
http://www.gov.yu/start.php?je=e&id=6
This official federation website presents an overview of Serbia and Montenegro's government and population.

Spangenburg, Ray, and Kit Moser. *The Crime of Genocide: Terror Against Humanity*. Berkeley Heights, NJ: Enslow Publishers, 2000.
This book takes a look at the causes and the devastating effects of genocide, examining twentieth-century examples including the ethnic cleansing that took place in the former Yugoslavia.

United Nations Mission in Kosovo.
http://www.unmikonline.org/
This website provides background information and updates on the situation in Kosovo and the UN's work there.

vgsbooks.com
http://www.vgsbooks.com
Visit vgsbooks.com, the home page of the Visual Geography Series®. You can get linked to all sorts of useful online information, including geographical, historical, demographic, cultural, and economic websites. The vgsbooks.com site is a great resource for late-breaking news and statistics.

Captions for photos appearing on cover and chapter openers:

Cover: A bell tower in Kotor overlooks Kotor Bay in Montenegro.

pp. 4–5 A happy crowd in Poderica, Montenegro, celebrates Montenegrins' 2006 vote to leave the federation with Serbia.

pp. 8–9 Commercial crops of sunflowers brighten the fertile plains of Vojvodina, Serbia. The region exports sunflower meal for cattle feed to other European nations.

pp. 18–19 Limestone caves in the karst region of Serbia and Montenegro sheltered the area's earliest inhabitants. Evidence shows humans first lived in the area in about 6000 B.C.

pp. 36–37 A crowd gathers in an antigovernment protest in central Belgrade, which is the nation's capital and home to 15 percent of Serbia and Montenegro's population.

pp. 44–45 Belgrade's Saint Mark's, a Serbian Orthodox cathedral, was built in the 1930s. It closely copies a Byzantine style of architecture.

Photo Acknowledgments

The images in this book are used with the permission of: © KOCA SULEJ-MANOVIC/epa/Corbis, pp. 4–5; © XNR Productions, pp. 6, 12; © Adam Radosavljevic, pp. 8–9, 18–19, 31, 35, 39, 40, 49, 50, 60, 62, 63; © George Spenceley/Art Directors, p. 11; © Steven S. Miric/SuperStock, p. 15; © Dejan Vjestica, pp. 17, 64; Federal Committee for Information, Belgrade, pp. 21, 29; © Hulton Archive/Getty Images, p. 24; Library of Congress, p. 26 (LC-DIG-ggbain-50222); © Les Stone/ZUMA Press, p. 32 (top); © Djordje Popovic/Red Dot/ZUMA Press, p. 32 (bottom); © GERARD CERLES/AFP/Getty Images, p. 34; © Reuters/CORBIS, pp. 36–37; © David Greedy/Newsmakers/Getty Images, p. 41; © Docevoc Velimir/Art Directors, pp. 44–45, 52; © ArtPhoto/www.diomedia.com, p. 47; © ANDREJ ISAKOVIC/AFP/Getty Images, p. 54; © DON EMMERT/AFP/Getty Images, p. 55; © Branislav Strugar/www.diomedia.com, p. 59; © DEV/www.diomedia.com, p. 61; Audrius Tomonis—www.banknotes.com, p. 68; © Laura Westlund/Independent Picture Service, p. 69.

Front cover: © Gill Copeland/Art Directors. Back cover: NASA.